QUILTER'S MIX and MATCH BLOCKS

OVER 200 PROJECT IDEAS

A Comprehensive Handbook

Fill your home with beautiful quilted creations! All you have to do is pick your project (we've included handy tables for all size of quilts), pick your favorite block or blocks, and get started. The finished size of each of the 50 classic blocks is 12", so it's easy to choose any combination of blocks. Mix and match the blocks to your heart's content!

Need some inspiration? Our four projects cover a variety of finishing and arrangement options. Convenient tables make quick work of figuring how many blocks you'll need for any size quilt. You'll also have information on borders, sashings, setting squares and triangles, and pillow finishing at your fingertips.

Turn to this handbook first when planning a new quilt. It's sure to become your best quilting friend!

LEISURE ARTS, INC.
Little Rock, Arkansas

THANK YOU

We greatly appreciate Julie Schrader for her expert machine quilting. We also thank our talented pattern testers who pieced and finished the projects: Larcie Burnett, Nelwyn Gray, Valerie Schramel, and Glenda Taylor.

EDITORIAL STAFF

Vice President and Editor-in-Chief: Sandra Graham Case. *Executive Director of Publications:* Cheryl Nodine Gunnells. *Senior Publications Director:* Susan White Sullivan. *Leaflets Publications Director:* Mary Sullivan Hutcheson. *Editorial Director:* Susan Frantz Wiles. *Photography Director:* Karen Hall. *Art Operations Director:* Jeff Curtis. TECHNICAL — *Technical Editor:* Lisa Lancaster. *Technical Writer:* Frances Huddleston. ART — *Art Publications Director:* Rhonda Shelby. *Art Imaging Director:* Mark Hawkins. *Art Category Manager and Lead Graphic Artist:* Lora Puls. *Graphic Artists:* Stephanie Hamling, Dayle Carozza, and Laura Atkins. *Photostylist:* Cassie Newsome. *Staff Photographer:* Andrew Uilkie. *Publishing Systems Administrator:* Becky Riddle. *Publishing Systems Assistants:* Clint Hanson, John Rose, and Chris Wertenberger. DESIGN — *Lead Designer:* Linda Tiano.

BUSINESS STAFF

Publisher: Rick Barton. *Vice President, Finance:* Tom Siebenmorgen. *Director of Corporate Planning and Development:* Laticia Dittrich. *Vice President, Retail Marketing:* Bob Humphrey. *Vice President, Sales:* Ray Shelgosh. *Vice President, National Accounts:* Pam Stebbins. *Director of Sales and Services:* Margaret Reinold. *Vice President, Operations:* Jim Dittrich. *Comptroller, Operations:* Rob Thieme. *Retail Customer Service Manager:* Stan Raynor. *Print Production Manager:* Fred F. Pruss.

Made in the United States of America

ISBN 1-57486-429-7

10 9 8 7 6 5 4 3 2 1

TABLE OF CONTENTS

ARROW STAR

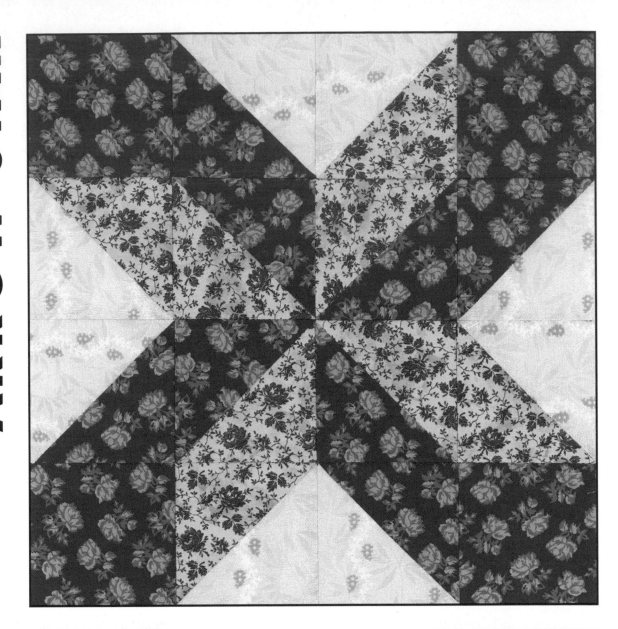

CUTTING OUT THE PIECES

From tan print fabric:
- Cut 4 **large squares** $3^7/8$" x $3^7/8$".

From light blue print fabric:
- Cut 4 **large squares** $3^7/8$" x $3^7/8$".

From dark blue fabric:
- Cut 4 **large squares** $3^7/8$" x $3^7/8$".
- Cut 4 **small squares** $3^1/2$" x $3^1/2$".

Use ¹/₄" seam allowances throughout.

1 Draw diagonal line (corner to corner) on wrong side of 4 tan **large squares** and 2 light blue **large squares**. With right sides together, place 1 tan **large square** on top of 1 dark blue **large square**. Stitch seam ¹/₄" from each side of drawn line (**Fig. 1**).

2 Cut along drawn line and press open to make 2 **Triangle-Squares**. Repeat with remaining **large squares** to make a total of 4 tan and dark blue **Triangle-Squares**, 4 tan and light blue **Triangles-Squares**, and 4 light blue and dark blue **Triangle-Squares**.

3 Sew 2 **small squares**, 1 tan and dark blue **Triangle-Square**, and 1 tan and light blue **Triangle-Square** together to make **Unit 1**. Make 2 **Unit 1's**.

Fig. 1

Triangle-Squares
(make 4)

(make 4)

(make 4)

Unit 1
(make 2)

ARROW STAR

4 Sew 2 light blue and dark blue **Triangle-Squares**, 1 tan and dark blue **Triangle-Square**, and 1 tan and light blue **Triangle-Square** together to make **Unit 2**. Make 2 **Unit 2's**.

5 Sew 2 **Unit 1's** and 2 **Unit 2's** together as shown in **Block Assembly** to complete **Block.**

Unit 2
(make 2)

Block Assembly

Block

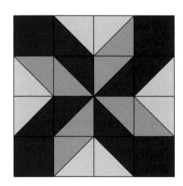

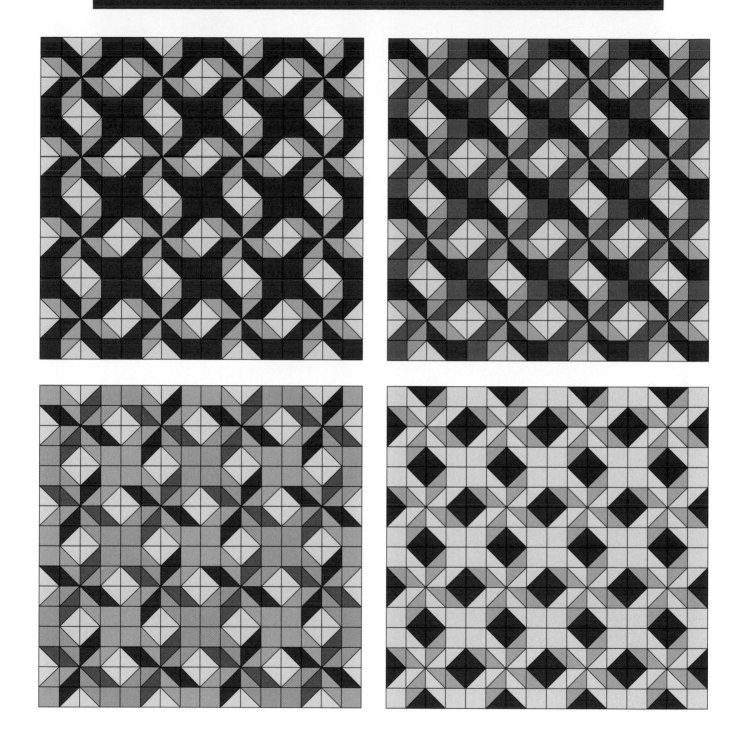

ARROW STAR

CUTTING OUT THE PIECES

From cream print fabric:
- Cut 4 **large squares** $3^7/_8$" x $3^7/_8$".
- Cut 5 **small squares** $3^1/_2$" x $3^1/_2$".
- Cut 1 square $3^7/_8$" x $3^7/_8$". Cut square *once* diagonally to make 2 **small triangles**.

From pink print fabric:
- Cut 3 **large squares** $3^7/_8$" x $3^7/_8$".

From gold print fabric:
- Cut 1 **large square** $3^7/_8$" x $3^7/_8$".
- Cut 1 square $6^7/_8$" x $6^7/_8$". Cut square *once* diagonally to make 2 **large triangles**. (You will use 1 and have 1 left over.)

Use ¹/₄" seam allowances throughout.

1 Draw diagonal line (corner to corner) on wrong side of each cream **large square**. With right sides together, place 1 cream **large square** on top of 1 pink **large square**. Stitch seam ¹/₄" from each side of drawn line (**Fig. 1**).

Fig. 1

Triangle-Squares
(make 6)

2 Cut along drawn line and press open to make 2 **Triangle-Squares**. Repeat with remaining **large squares** to make a total of 6 cream and pink **Triangle-Squares** and 2 cream and gold **Triangle-Squares**.

(make 2)

Unit 1

3 Sew 3 cream and pink **Triangle-Squares** and 1 **small square** together to make **Unit 1**.

Unit 2

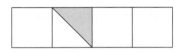

4 Sew 1 cream and gold **Triangle-Square** and 3 **small squares** together to make **Unit 2**.

Unit 3

5 Sew 1 cream and pink **Triangle-Square** and 2 **small triangles** together to make **Unit 3**.

BASKET

6 Sew **Unit 3** and 1 **large triangle** together to make **Unit 4**.

Unit 4

Unit 5

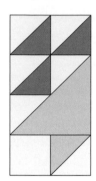

7 Sew 2 cream and pink **Triangle-Squares** together to make **Unit 5**.

Unit 6

Unit 7

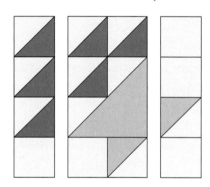

8 Sew 1 cream and gold **Triangle-Square** and 1 **small square** together to make **Unit 6**.

9 Sew **Unit 4**, **Unit 5**, and **Unit 6** together to make **Unit 7**.

Block Assembly

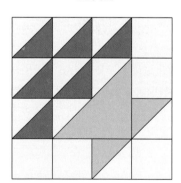

10 Sew **Unit 1**, **Unit 2**, and **Unit 7** together as shown in **Block Assembly** to complete **Block**.

Block

BASKET

CUTTING OUT THE PIECES

From cream print fabric:
- Cut 16 **small squares** $2^1/_2$" x $2^1/_2$".
- Cut 2 squares $4^7/_8$" x $4^7/_8$". Cut squares *once* diagonally to make 4 **large triangles**.

From pink print fabric:
- Cut 4 **rectangles** $4^1/_2$" x $2^1/_2$".

From green print fabric:
- Cut 4 **rectangles** $4^1/_2$" x $2^1/_2$".

From gold print fabric:
- Cut 1 **large square** $4^1/_2$" x $4^1/_2$".
- Cut 8 **small squares** $2^1/_2$" x $2^1/_2$".
- Cut 4 squares $2^7/_8$" x $2^7/_8$". Cut squares *once* diagonally to make 8 **small triangles**.

Use ¹/₄" seam allowances throughout.

1 Sew 1 cream **small square** and 2 **small triangles** together to make **Unit 1**. Make 4 **Unit 1's**.

Unit 1
(make 4)

2 Sew 1 **Unit 1** and 1 **large triangle** together to make **Unit 2**. Make 4 **Unit 2's**.

Unit 2
(make 4)

3 With right sides together, place 1 gold **small square** on 1 end of 1 green **rectangle** and stitch diagonally (**Fig. 1**). Trim ¹/₄" from stitching line (**Fig. 2**). Open up and press, pressing seam allowance to darker fabric (**Fig. 3**).

Fig. 1

Fig. 2

Fig. 3

Fig. 4

4 Place another gold **small square** on opposite end of **rectangle**. Stitch and trim as shown in **Fig. 4**. Open up and press to complete **Flying Geese Unit A**. Make 4 **Flying Geese Unit A's**.

Unit A
(make 4)

Unit B
(make 4)

5 Using cream **small squares** and pink **rectangles**, repeat Steps 3 and 4 to make 4 **Flying Geese Unit B's**.

Unit 3
(make 4)

6 Sew 1 **Flying Geese Unit A** and 1 **Flying Geese Unit B** together to make **Unit 3**. Make 4 **Unit 3's**.

BOXES

7 With right sides together, place 1 cream **small square** on 1 corner of **large square** and stitch diagonally (**Fig. 5**). Trim ¼" from stitching line (**Fig. 6**). Open up and press, pressing seam allowance to darker fabric (**Fig. 7**).

8 Continue adding cream **small squares** to corners of **large square** as shown in **Fig. 8**. Open up and press to complete **Unit 4**.

9 Sew 2 **Unit 2's** and 1 **Unit 3** together to make **Unit 5**. Make 2 **Unit 5's**.

10 Sew 2 **Unit 3's** and **Unit 4** together to make **Unit 6**.

11 Sew 2 **Unit 5's** and **Unit 6** together as shown in **Block Assembly** to complete **Block**.

Fig. 5

Fig. 6

Fig. 7

Fig. 8

Unit 4

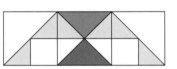

Unit 5
(make 2)

Unit 6

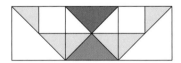

Block Assembly

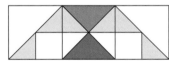

Block

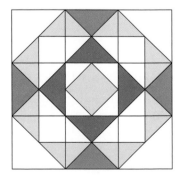

14

BOXES

CUTTING OUT THE PIECES

From cream print fabric:
- Cut 4 **large squares** $3^1/_2$" x $3^1/_2$".
- Cut 4 **small squares** 2" x 2".
- Cut 12 **rectangles** $3^1/_2$" x 2".

From gold print fabric:
- Cut 5 **large squares** $3^1/_2$" x $3^1/_2$".

From teal print fabric:
- Cut 32 **small squares** 2" x 2".

Use ¹/₄" seam allowances throughout.

1 With right sides together, place 1 teal **small square** on 1 end of 1 **rectangle** and stitch diagonally (**Fig. 1**). Trim ¹/₄" from stitching line (**Fig. 2**). Open up and press, pressing seam allowance to darker fabric (**Fig. 3**).

2 Place another teal **small square** on opposite end of **rectangle**. Stitch and trim as shown in **Fig. 4**. Open up and press to complete **Flying Geese Unit**. Make 8 **Flying Geese Units**.

3 Sew 2 **Flying Geese Units** and 1 cream **rectangle** together to make **Unit 1**. Make 2 **Unit 1's**.

4 Sew 1 **Unit 1** and 2 cream **small squares** together to make **Unit 2**. Make 2 **Unit 2's**.

5 With right sides together, place 1 teal **small square** on 1 corner of cream **large square** and stitch diagonally (**Fig. 5**). Trim ¹/₄" from stitching line (**Fig. 6**). Open up and press, pressing seam allowance to darker fabric (**Fig. 7**).

Fig. 1   Fig. 2

Fig. 3   Fig. 4

Flying Geese Unit
(make 8)

Unit 1
(make 2)

Unit 2
(make 2)

Fig.5   Fig. 6

Fig. 7

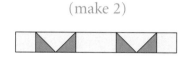

BRIGHT STARS

6 Continue adding teal **small squares** to corners of cream **large square** as shown in **Fig. 8**. Open up and press to complete **Unit 3**. Make 4 **Unit 3's**.

7 Sew 2 **Flying Geese Units**, 2 gold **large squares**, and 1 **Unit 3** together to make **Unit 4**. Make 2 **Unit 4's**.

8 Sew 2 **rectangles**, 2 **Unit 3's,** and 1 gold **large square** together to make **Unit 5**.

9 Sew 2 **Unit 2's**, 2 **Unit 4's,** and **Unit 5** together as shown in **Block Assembly** to complete **Block**.

Fig. 8

Unit 3
(make 4)

Unit 4
(make 2)

Unit 5

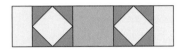

Block Assembly

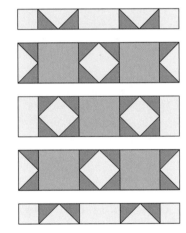

Block

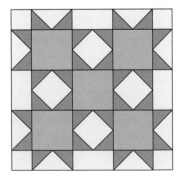

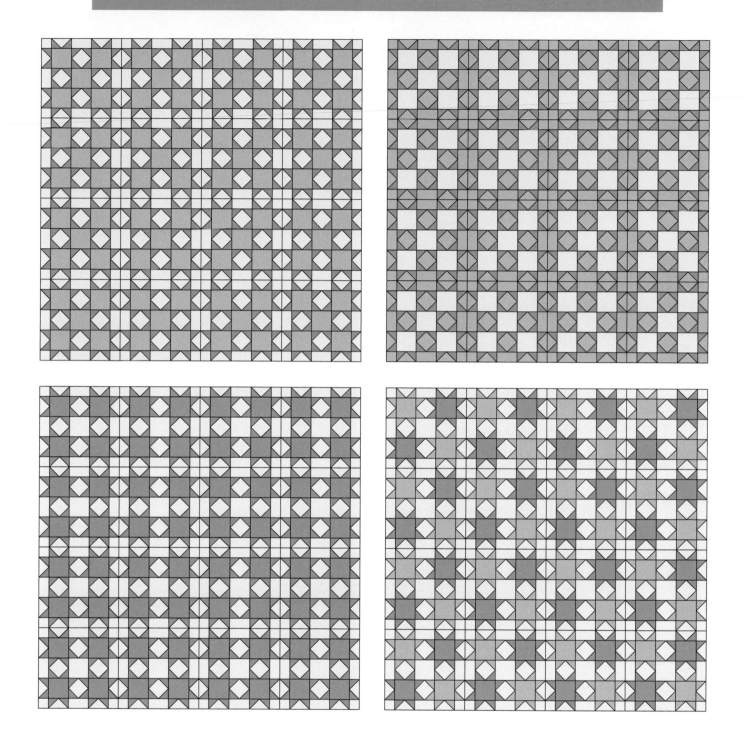

BRIGHT STARS

CUTTING OUT THE PIECES

From cream print fabric:
- Cut 2 **large squares** $4^7/8$" x $4^7/8$".
- Cut 1 **medium square** $4^1/2$" x $4^1/2$".
- Cut 8 **rectangles** $4^1/2$" x $2^1/2$".

From blue print fabric:
- Cut 16 **small squares** $2^1/2$" x $2^1/2$".

From gold print fabric:
- Cut 2 **large squares** $4^7/8$" x $4^7/8$".

Use ¹/₄" seam allowances throughout.

1 Draw diagonal line (corner to corner) on wrong side of each cream **large square**. With right sides together, place 1 cream **large square** on top of 1 gold **large square**. Stitch seam ¹/₄" from each side of drawn line (**Fig. 1**).

2 Cut along drawn line and press open to make 2 **Triangle-Squares**. Make 4 **Triangle-Squares**.

3 With right sides together, place 1 **small square** on 1 end of 1 **rectangle** and stitch diagonally (**Fig. 2**). Trim ¹/₄" from stitching line (**Fig. 3**). Open up and press, pressing seam allowance to darker fabric (**Fig. 4**).

4 Place another **small square** on opposite end of **rectangle**. Stitch and trim as shown in **Fig. 5**. Open up and press to complete **Flying Geese Unit**. Make 8 **Flying Geese Units**.

Fig. 1

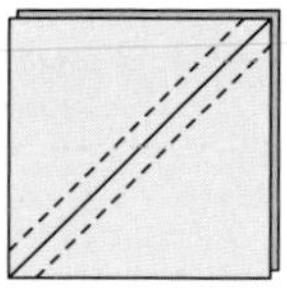

Triangle-Squares
(make 4)

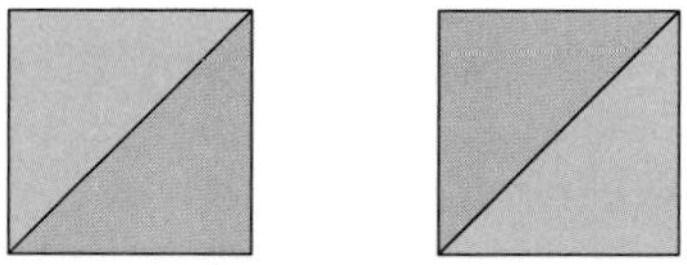

Fig. 2

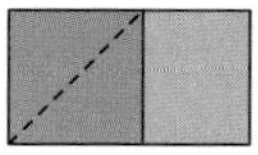

Fig. 3

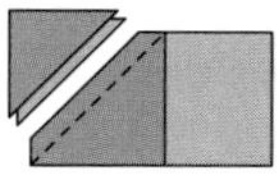

Fig. 4

Fig. 5

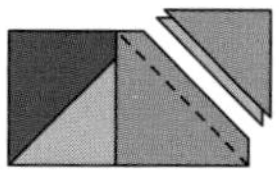

Flying Geese Unit
(make 8)

CAPITAL T

5 Sew 2 **Flying Geese Units** together to make **Unit 1**. Make 4 **Unit 1's**.

6 Sew 2 **Triangle-Squares** and 1 **Unit 1** together to make **Unit 2**. Make 2 **Unit 2's**.

7 Sew 2 **Unit 1's** and **medium square** together to make **Unit 3**.

8 Sew 2 **Unit 2's** and **Unit 3** together as shown in **Block Assembly** to complete **Block**.

Unit 1
(make 4)

Unit 2
(make 2)

Unit 3

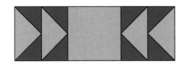

Block Assembly

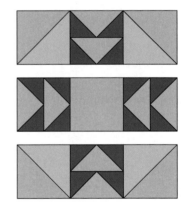

Block

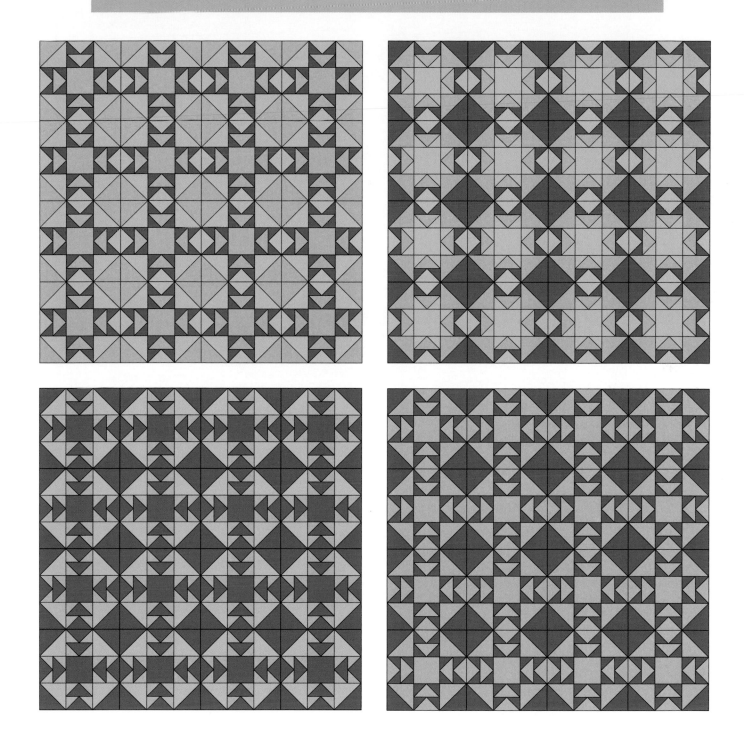

CAPITAL T

CARD TRICK

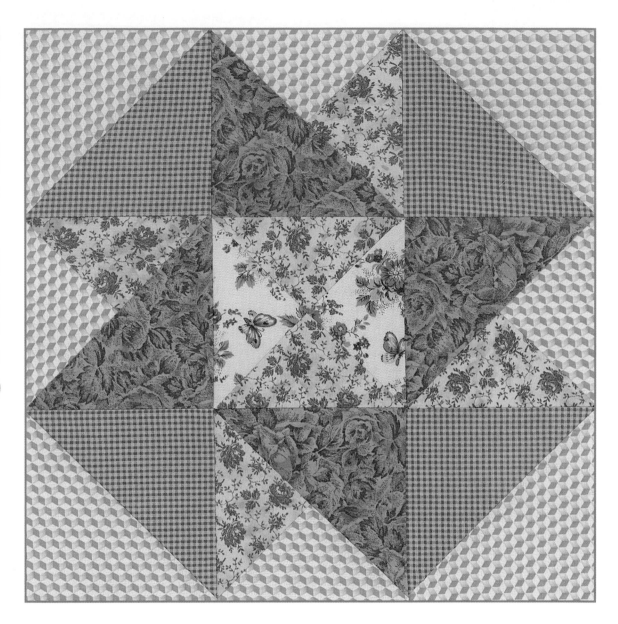

CUTTING OUT THE PIECES

From tan print fabric:
- Cut 2 **squares** $4^7/8$" x $4^7/8$".
- Cut 1 square $5^1/4$" x $5^1/4$". Cut square *twice* diagonally to make 4 **small triangles**.

From gold print fabric:
- Cut 1 square $5^1/4$" x $5^1/4$". Cut square *twice* diagonally to make 4 **small triangles**. (You will use 2 and have 2 left over.)

From rust checked fabric:
- Cut 2 **squares** $4^7/8$" x $4^7/8$".

From dark rust print fabric:
- Cut 2 squares $4^7/8$" x $4^7/8$". Cut squares *once* diagonally to make 4 **large triangles**.

From light rust print fabric:
- Cut 2 squares $5^1/4$" x $5^1/4$". Cut squares *twice* diagonally to make 8 **small triangles**. (You will use 6 and have 2 left over.)

Use ¹/₄" seam allowances throughout.

1 Draw diagonal line (corner to corner) on wrong side of each tan **square**. With right sides together, place 1 tan **square** on top of 1 rust checked **square**. Stitch seam ¹/₄" from each side of drawn line (**Fig. 1**).

2 Cut along drawn line and press open to make 2 **Triangle-Squares**. Make 4 **Triangle-Squares**.

3 Sew 1 tan **small triangle** and 1 light rust **small triangle** together to make **Unit 1**. Make 4 **Unit 1's**.

4 Sew 1 **Unit 1** and 1 **large triangle** together to make **Unit 2**. Make 4 **Unit 2's**.

5 Sew 1 gold **small triangle** and 1 light rust **small triangle** together to make **Unit 3**. Make 2 **Unit 3's**.

Fig. 1

Triangle-Squares
(make 4)

Unit 1
(make 4)

Unit 2
(make 4)

Unit 3
(make 2)

CARD TRICK

6 Sew 2 **Unit 3's** together to make **Hourglass Unit**.

Hourglass Unit

7 Sew 2 **Triangle-Squares** and 1 **Unit 2** together to make **Unit 4**. Make 2 **Unit 4's**.

Unit 4
(make 2)

8 Sew 2 **Unit 2's** and **Hourglass Unit** together to make **Unit 5**.

Unit 5
(make 2)

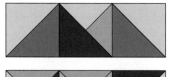

9 Sew 2 **Unit 4's** and **Unit 5** together as shown in **Block Assembly** to complete **Block**.

Block Assembly

Block

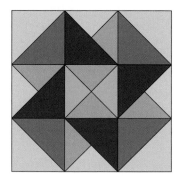

CARD TRICK

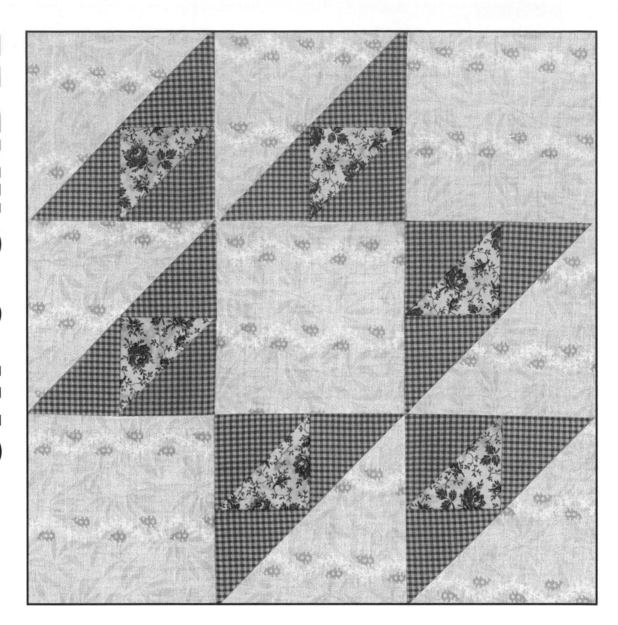

CUTTING OUT THE PIECES

From cream print fabric:
- Cut 3 **large squares** $4^1/_2$" x $4^1/_2$".
- Cut 3 squares $4^7/_8$" x $4^7/_8$". Cut squares *once* diagonally to make 6 **large triangles**.

From burgundy print fabric:
- Cut 3 **small squares** $2^7/_8$" x $2^7/_8$".

From burgundy checked fabric:
- Cut 3 **small squares** $2^7/_8$" x $2^7/_8$".
- Cut 6 squares $2^7/_8$" x $2^7/_8$". Cut squares *once* diagonally to make 12 **small triangles**.

Use ¹/₄" seam allowances throughout.

1 Draw diagonal line (corner to corner) on wrong side of each burgundy print **small square**. With right sides together, place 1 burgundy print **small square** on top of 1 burgundy checked **small square**. Stitch seam ¹/₄" from each side of drawn line (**Fig. 1**).

Fig. 1

Triangle Squares
(make 6)

2 Cut along drawn line and press open to make 2 **Triangle-Squares**. Make 6 **Triangle-Squares**.

Unit 1
(make 6)

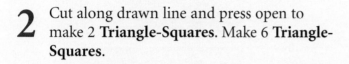

3 Sew 1 **triangle-square** and 2 **small triangles** together to make **Unit 1**. Make 6 **Unit 1's**.

Unit 2
(make 6)

4 Sew 1 **Unit 1** and 1 **large triangle** together to make **Unit 2**. Make 6 **Unit 2's**.

CAT'S CRADLE

5 Sew 2 **Unit 2's** and 1 **large square** together to make **Unit 3**. Make 2 **Unit 3's**.

6 Sew 2 **Unit 2's** and 1 **large square** together to make **Unit 4**.

7 Sew 2 **Unit 3's** and **Unit 4** together as shown in **Block Assembly** to complete **Block**.

Unit 3
(make 2)

Unit 4

Block Assembly

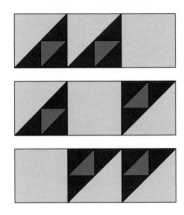

Block

CAT'S CRADLE

CHAIN

CUTTING OUT THE PIECES

From cream print fabric:
- Cut 2 **large squares** $4^1/_2$" x $4^1/_2$".
- Cut 16 **small squares** $2^1/_2$" x $2^1/_2$".

From burgundy print fabric:
- Cut 2 **large squares** $4^1/_2$" x $4^1/_2$".
- Cut 4 **small squares** $2^1/_2$" x $2^1/_2$".

From green print fabric:
- Cut 4 **rectangles** $4^1/_2$" x $2^1/_2$".

Use ¼" seam allowances throughout.

1 With right sides together, place 1 cream **small square** on 1 end of 1 **rectangle** and stitch diagonally (**Fig. 1**). Trim ¼" from stitching line (**Fig. 2**). Open up and press, pressing seam allowance to darker fabric (**Fig. 3**).

2 Place another cream **small square** on opposite end of **rectangle**. Stitch and trim as shown in **Fig. 4**. Open up and press to complete **Flying Geese Unit**. Make 4 **Flying Geese Units**.

3 Sew 1 **Flying Geese Unit** and 2 cream **small squares** together to make **Unit 1**. Make 4 **Unit 1's**.

4 Sew 1 **Unit 1** and 2 burgundy **small squares** together to make **Unit 2**. Make 2 **Unit 2's**.

Fig. 1

Fig. 2

Fig. 3

Fig. 4

Flying Geese Unit
(make 4)

Unit 1
(make 4)

Unit 2
(make 2)

CHAIN

5 Sew 2 burgundy **large squares** and 2 cream **large squares** together to make **Unit 3**.

6 Sew **Unit 3** and 2 **Unit 1's** together to make **Unit 4**.

7 Sew **Unit 4** and 2 **Unit 2's** together as shown in **Block Assembly** to complete **Block**.

Unit 3

Unit 4

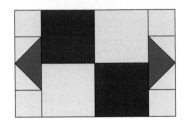

Block Assembly

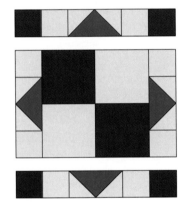

Block

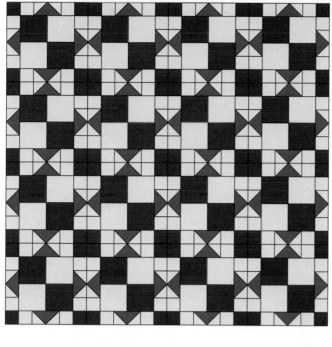

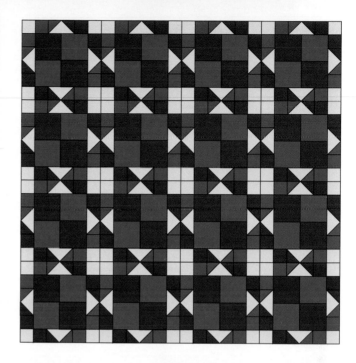

CHAIN

CHECKERBOARD

CUTTING OUT THE PIECES

From cream print fabric:
- Cut 36 **small squares** $2^1/2$" x $2^1/2$".

From red print fabric:
- Cut 2 **large squares** $4^1/2$" x $4^1/2$".

From gold print fabric:
- Cut 2 **large squares** $4^1/2$" x $4^1/2$".

From blue print fabric:
- Cut 2 **large squares** $4^1/2$" x $4^1/2$".

From green print fabric:
- Cut 2 **large squares** $4^1/2$" x $4^1/2$".

From brown print fabric:
- Cut 1 **large square** $4^1/2$" x $4^1/2$".

Use ¹/₄" seam allowances throughout.

1 With right sides together, place 1 **small square** on 1 corner of 1 red **large square** and stitch diagonally (**Fig. 1**). Trim ¹/₄" from stitching line (**Fig. 2**). Open up and press, pressing seam allowance to darker fabric (**Fig. 3**).

2 Continue adding **small squares** to corners of red **large square** as shown in **Fig. 4**. Open up and press to complete **Red Unit 1**. Make 2 **Red Unit 1's**.

3 Repeat Steps 1 and 2 to make 2 **Gold Unit 1's**, 2 **Blue Unit 1's**, 2 **Green Unit 1's**, and 1 **Brown Unit 1**.

Fig. 1

Fig. 2

Fig. 3

Fig. 4

Red Unit 1
(make 2)

Gold Unit 1
(make 2)

Blue Unit 1
(make 2)

Green Unit 1
(make 2)

Brown Unit 1
(make 1)

CHECKERBOARD

4 Sew 1 **Red Unit 1**, 1 **Gold Unit 1**, and 1 **Blue Unit 1** together to make **Unit 2**. Make 2 **Unit 2's**.

5 Sew 2 **Green Unit 1's** and **Brown Unit 1** together to make **Unit 3**.

6 Sew 2 **Unit 2's** and **Unit 3** together as shown in **Block Assembly** to complete **Block**.

Unit 2
(make 2)

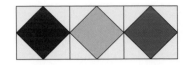

Unit 3

Block Assembly

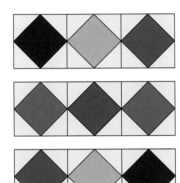

Block

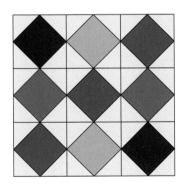

CHECKERBOARD

CHURN DASH

CUTTING OUT THE PIECES

From tan small print fabric:
- Cut 2 **large squares** $4^7/_8$" x $4^7/_8$".
- Cut 1 **small square** $4^1/_2$" x $4^1/_2$".

From tan large print fabric:
- Cut 4 **rectangles** $4^1/_2$" x $2^1/_2$".

From orange print fabric:
- Cut 4 **rectangles** $4^1/_2$" x $2^1/_2$".

From blue print fabric:
- Cut 2 **large squares** $4^7/_8$" x $4^7/_8$".

40

Use ¹/₄" seam allowances throughout.

1 Draw diagonal line (corner to corner) on wrong side of each tan small print **large square**. With right sides together, place 1 tan small print **large square** on top of 1 blue **large square**. Stitch seam ¹/₄" from each side of drawn line (**Fig. 1**).

2 Cut along drawn line and press open to make 2 **Triangle-Squares**. Make 4 **Triangle-Squares**.

3 Sew 1 tan large print **rectangle** and 1 orange **rectangle** together to make **Unit 1**. Make 4 **Unit 1's**.

4 Sew 2 **Triangle-Squares** and 1 **Unit 1** together to make **Unit 2**. Make **2 Unit 2's**.

Fig. 1

Triangle-Squares
(make 4)

Unit 1
(make 4)

Unit 2
(make 2)

CHURN DASH

5 Sew 2 **Unit 1's** and **small square** together to make **Unit 3**.

6 Sew 2 **Unit 2's** and **Unit 3** together as shown in **Block Assembly** to complete **Block**.

Unit 3

Block Assembly

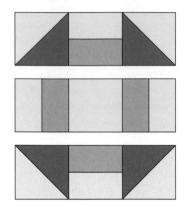

Block

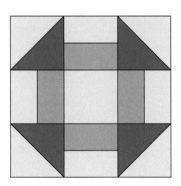

CHURN DASH

CORN AND BEANS

CUTTING OUT THE PIECES

From tan print fabric:
- Cut 14 **large squares** $2^7/8"$ x $2^7/8"$.
- Cut 6 **small squares** $2^1/2"$ x $2^1/2"$.

From blue print fabric:
- Cut 14 **large squares** $2^7/8"$ x $2^7/8"$.
- Cut 2 **small squares** $2^1/2"$ x $2^1/2"$.

Use ¼" seam allowances throughout.

1 Draw diagonal line (corner to corner) on wrong side of each tan **large square**. With right sides together, place 1 tan **large square** on top of 1 blue **large square**. Stitch seam ¼" from each side of drawn line (**Fig. 1**).

2 Cut along drawn line and press open to make 2 **Triangle-Squares**. Make 28 **Triangle-Squares**.

3 Sew 2 **Triangle-Squares** and 1 blue **small square** together to make **Unit 1**. Make 2 **Unit 1's**.

4 Sew 3 **Triangle-Squares** together to make **Unit 2**. Make 2 **Unit 2's**.

5 Sew 2 **Triangle-Squares** and 1 tan **small square** together to make **Unit 3**. Make 2 **Unit 3's**.

6 Sew 1 **Unit 1**, 1 **Unit 2**, and 1 **Unit 3** together to make **Unit 4**. Make 2 **Unit 4's**.

Fig. 1

Triangle-squares
(make 28)

Unit 1
(make 2)

Unit 2
(make 2)

Unit 3
(make 2)

Unit 4
(make 2)

CORN AND BEANS

7 Sew 2 **Triangle-Squares** and 1 tan **small square** together to make **Unit 5**. Make 2 **Unit 5's**.

8 Sew 3 **Triangle-Squares** together to make **Unit 6**. Make 2 **Unit 6's**.

9 Sew 2 **Triangle-Squares** and 1 tan **small square** together to make **Unit 7**. Make 2 **Unit 7's**.

10 Sew 1 **Unit 5**, 1 **Unit 6**, and 1 **Unit 7** together to make **Unit 8**. Make 2 **Unit 8's**.

11 Sew 2 **Unit 4's** and 2 **Unit 8's** together as shown in **Block Assembly** to complete **Block**.

Unit 5
(make 2)

Unit 6
(make 2)

Unit 7
(make 2)

Unit 8
(make 2)

Block Assembly

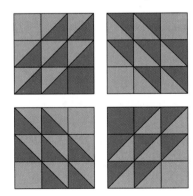

Block

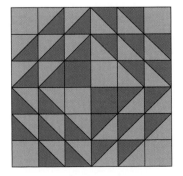

CORN AND BEANS

CROSSES AND LOSSES

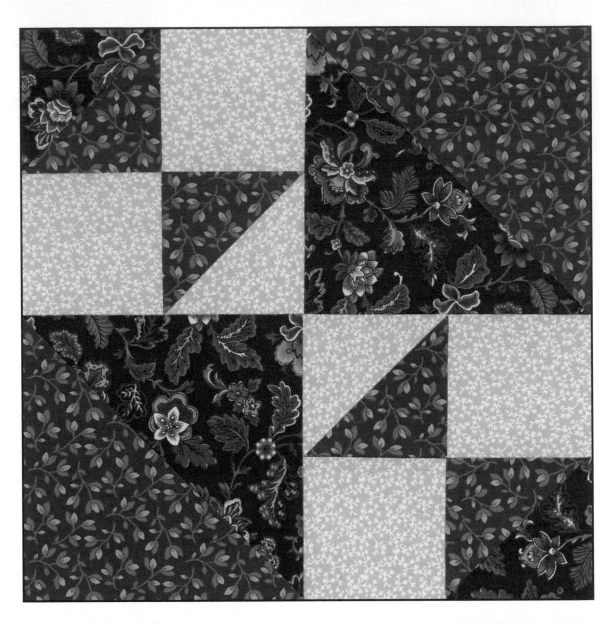

CUTTING OUT THE PIECES

From cream print fabric:
- Cut 1 **medium square** $3^7/8$" x $3^7/8$".
- Cut 4 **small squares** $3^1/2$" x $3^1/2$".

From green print fabric:
- Cut 1 **large square** $6^7/8$" x $6^7/8$".
- Cut 2 **medium squares** $3^7/8$" x $3^7/8$".

From red print fabric:
- Cut 1 **large square** $6^7/8$" x $6^7/8$".
- Cut 1 **medium square** $3^7/8$" x $3^7/8$".

Use ¹/₄" seam allowances throughout.

1 Draw diagonal line (corner to corner) on wrong side of each green **medium square**. With right sides together, place 1 green **medium square** on top of cream **medium square**. Stitch seam ¹/₄" from each side of drawn line (**Fig. 1**).

2 Cut along drawn line and press open to make 2 **Small Triangle-Squares**. Make 2 green and cream **Small Triangle-Squares** and 2 green and red **Small Triangle-Squares**.

3 Repeat Steps 1 and 2 using **large squares** to make 2 green and red **Large Triangle-Squares**.

4 Sew 1 green and cream **Small Triangle-Square** and 1 **small square** together to make **Unit 1**. Make 2 **Unit 1's**.

Fig. 1

Small Triangle-Squares
(make 2)

(make 2)

Large Triangle-Squares
(make 2)

Unit 1
(make 2)

CROSSES AND LOSSES

5 Sew 1 green and red **Small Triangle-Square** and 1 **small square** together to make **Unit 2**. Make 2 **Unit 2's.**

6 Sew 1 **Unit 1** and 1 **Unit 2** together to make **Unit 3**. Make 2 **Unit 3's.**

7 Sew 2 **Large Triangle-Squares** and 2 **Unit 3's** together as shown in **Block Assembly** to complete **Block**.

Unit 2
(make 2)

Unit 3
(make 2)

Block Assembly

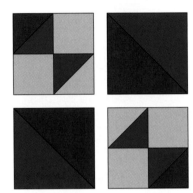

Block

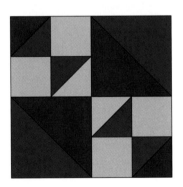

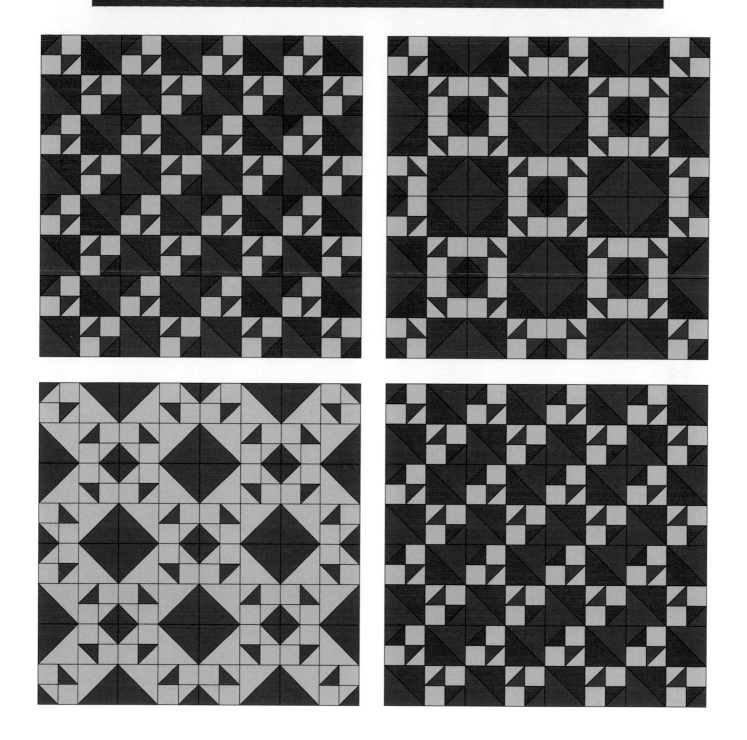

51

CROW'S FOOT

CUTTING OUT THE PIECES

From cream print fabric:
- Cut 4 **medium squares** $2^3/_8$" x $2^3/_8$".
- Cut 16 **small squares** 2" x 2".
- Cut 4 **rectangles** $3^1/_2$" x 2".

From light burgundy floral fabric:
- Cut 5 **large squares** $3^1/_2$" x $3^1/_2$".

From dark burgundy floral fabric:
- Cut 4 **medium squares** $2^3/_8$" x $2^3/_8$".
- Cut 8 **rectangles** $3^1/_2$" x 2".

From burgundy checked fabric:
- Cut 12 **small squares** 2" x 2".

Use ¼" seam allowances throughout.

1 Draw diagonal line (corner to corner) on wrong side of each cream **medium square**. With right sides together, place 1 cream **medium square** on top of 1 dark burgundy floral **medium square**. Stitch seam ¼" from each side of drawn line (**Fig. 1**).

2 Cut along drawn line and press open to make 2 **Triangle-Squares**. Make 8 **Triangle-Squares**.

3 With right sides together, place 1 burgundy checked **small square** on 1 end of 1 cream **rectangle** and stitch diagonally (**Fig. 2**). Trim ¼" from stitching line (**Fig. 3**). Open up and press, pressing seam allowance to darker fabric (**Fig. 4**).

4 Place another burgundy checked **small square** on opposite end of **rectangle**. Stitch and trim as shown in **Fig. 5**. Open up and press to complete **Flying Geese Unit A**. Make 4 **Flying Geese Unit A's**.

5 Repeat Steps 3 and 4 using cream **small squares** and dark burgundy floral **rectangles** to make 4 **Flying Geese Unit B's**.

Fig. 1

Triangle-Squares
(make 8)

Fig. 2

Fig. 3

Fig. 4

Fig. 5

Flying Geese Unit A
(make 4)

Flying Geese Unit B
(make 4)

CROW'S FOOT

6 Sew 1 **Flying Geese Unit A** and 1 dark burgundy floral **rectangle** together to make **Unit 1**. Make 4 **Unit 1's**.

7 Sew 1 **Triangle-Square** and 1 cream **small square** together to make **Unit 2a**. Make 4 **Unit 2a's** and 4 **Unit 2b's**.

8 Sew 1 **Unit 2a**, 1 **Unit 2b**, 2 burgundy checked **small squares**, and 1 **Flying Geese Unit B** together to make **Unit 3**. Make 2 **Unit 3's**.

9 Sew 1 **Unit 1**, 1 **Unit 2a**, 1 **Unit 2b**, and 2 **large squares** together to make **Unit 4**. Make 2 **Unit 4's**.

10 Sew 2 **Unit 1's**, 2 **Flying Geese Units B's**, and 1 **large square** together to make **Unit 5**.

11 Sew 2 **Unit 3's**, 2 **Unit 4's**, and **Unit 5** together as shown in **Block Assembly** to complete **Block**.

Unit 1
(make 4)

Unit 2a
(make 4)

Unit 2b
(make 4)

Unit 3
(make 2)

Unit 4
(make 2)

Unit 5

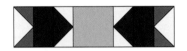

Block Assembly

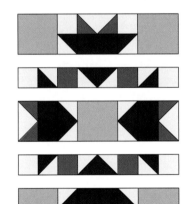

Block

54

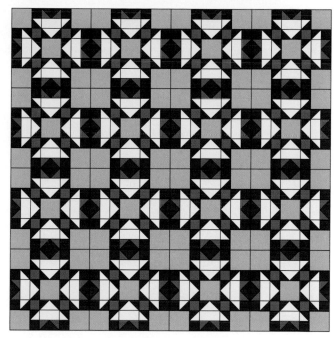

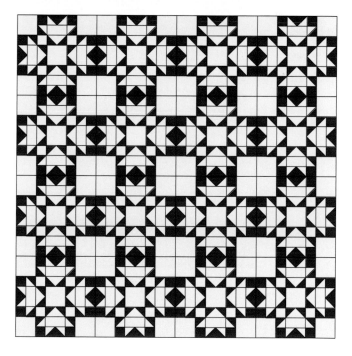

CROW'S FOOT

CUT GLASS DISH

CUTTING OUT THE PIECES

From cream print fabric:
- Cut 12 **small squares** $2^7/8$" x $2^7/8$".

From green print fabric:
- Cut 3 **large squares** $4^1/2$" x $4^1/2$".

From burgundy print fabric:
- Cut 12 **small squares** $2^7/8$" x $2^7/8$".

ASSEMBLING THE BLOCK

Use ¹/₄" seam allowances throughout.

1 Draw diagonal line (corner to corner) on wrong side of each cream **small square**. With right sides together, place 1 cream **small square** on top of 1 burgundy **small square**. Stitch seam ¹/₄" from each side of drawn line (**Fig. 1**).

2 Cut along drawn line and press open to make 2 **Triangle-Squares**. Make 24 **Triangle-Squares**.

3 Sew 4 **Triangle-Squares** together to make **Unit 1**. Make 6 **Unit 1's**.

4 Sew 2 **Unit 1's** and 1 **large square** together to make **Unit 2**. Make 2 **Unit 2's**.

Fig. 1

Triangle-Squares
(make 24)

Unit 1
(make 6)

Unit 2
(make 2)

CUT GLASS DISH

5 Sew 2 **Unit 1's** and 1 **large square** together to make **Unit 3**.

6 Sew 2 **Unit 2's** and **Unit 3** together as shown in **Block Assembly** to complete **Block**.

Unit 3

Block Assembly

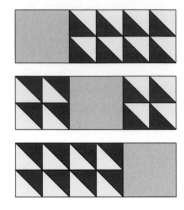

Block

CUT GLASS DISH

DOUBLE X

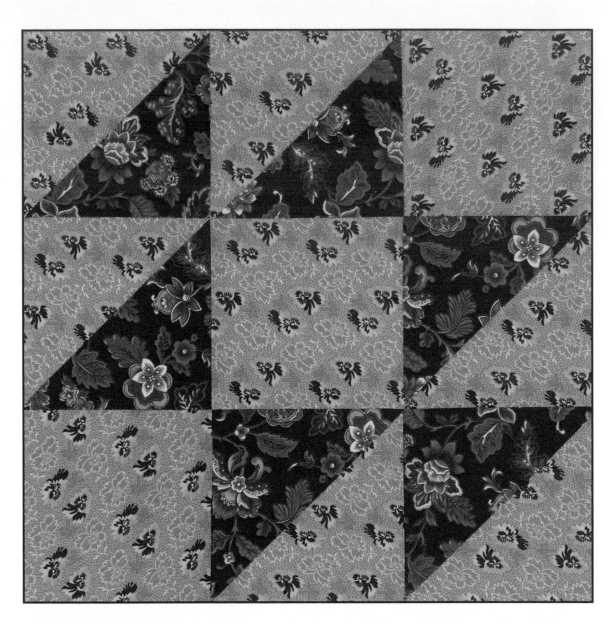

CUTTING OUT THE PIECES

From green print fabric:
- Cut 3 **large squares** $4^7/_8$" x $4^7/_8$".
- Cut 3 **small squares** $4^1/_2$" x $4^1/_2$".

From red print fabric:
- Cut 3 **large squares** $4^7/_8$" x $4^7/_8$".

Use ¹/₄" seam allowances throughout.

1 Draw diagonal line (corner to corner) on wrong side of each green **large square**. With right sides together, place 1 green **large square** on top of 1 red **large square**. Stitch seam ¹/₄" from each side of drawn line (**Fig. 1**).

2 Cut along drawn line and press open to make 2 **Triangle-Squares**. Make 6 **Triangle-Squares**.

3 Sew 2 **Triangle-Squares** and 1 **small square** together to make **Unit 1**. Make 2 **Unit 1's**.

Fig. 1

Triangle-Squares
(make 6)

Unit 1
(make 2)

DOUBLE X

4 Sew 2 **Triangle-Squares** and 1 **small square** together to make **Unit 2.**

5 Sew 2 **Unit 1's** and **Unit 2** together as shown in **Block Assembly** to complete **Block.**

Unit 2

Block Assembly

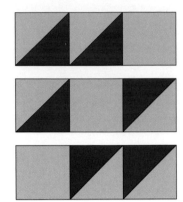

Block

DOUBLE X

DOVE-IN-THE-WINDOW

CUTTING OUT THE PIECES

From cream print fabric:
- Cut 2 **medium squares** $2^7/8$" x $2^7/8$".
- Cut 4 squares $2^7/8$" x $2^7/8$". Cut squares *once* diagonally to make 8 **small triangles**.
- Cut 8 **rectangles** $4^1/2$" x $2^1/2$".

From tan print fabric:
- Cut 1 **large square** $4^1/2$" x $4^1/2$".

From orange print fabric:
- Cut 2 **medium squares** $2^7/8$" x $2^7/8$".
- Cut 8 **small squares** $2^1/2$" x $2^1/2$".
- Cut 2 squares $4^7/8$" x $4^7/8$". Cut squares *once* diagonally to make 4 **large triangles**.

Use ¹/₄" seam allowances throughout.

1 Draw diagonal line (corner to corner) on wrong side of each cream **medium square**. With right sides together, place 1 cream **medium square** on top of 1 orange **medium square**. Stitch seam ¹/₄" from each side of drawn line (**Fig. 1**).

2 Cut along drawn line and press open to make 2 **Triangle-Squares**. Make 4 **Triangle-Squares**.

3 Sew 1 **Triangle-Square** and 2 **small triangles** together to make **Unit 1**. Make 4 **Unit 1's**.

4 Sew **Unit 1** and 1 **large triangle** together to make **Unit 2**. Make 4 **Unit 2's**.

5 With right sides together, place 1 **small square** on 1 end of 1 **rectangle** and stitch diagonally (**Fig. 2**). Trim ¹/₄" from stitching line (**Fig. 3**). Open up and press, pressing seam allowance to darker fabric (**Fig. 4**).

Fig. 1

Triangle-Squares
(make 4)

Unit 1
(make 4)

Unit 2
(make 4)

Fig. 2

Fig. 3

Fig. 4

DOVE-IN-THE-WINDOW

6 Place another **small square** on opposite end of **rectangle**. Stitch and trim as shown in **Fig. 5**. Open up and press to complete **Flying Geese Unit**. Make 4 **Flying Geese Units**.

7 Sew 1 **Flying Geese Unit** and 1 **rectangle** together to make **Unit 3**. Make 4 **Unit 3's**.

8 Sew 2 **Unit 2's** and 1 **Unit 3** together to make **Unit 4**. Make 2 **Unit 4's**.

9 Sew 2 **Unit 3's** and **large square** together to make **Unit 5**.

10 Sew 2 **Unit 4's** and **Unit 5** together as shown in **Block Assembly** to complete **Block**.

Fig. 5

Flying Geese Unit
(make 4)

Unit 3
(make 4)

Unit 4
(make 2)

Unit 5

Block Assembly

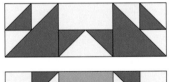

Block

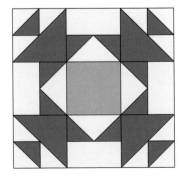

DOVE-IN-THE-WINDOW

DUBLIN STEPS

CUTTING OUT THE PIECES

From cream print fabric:
- Cut 6 **small squares** $2^1/_2$" x $2^1/_2$".
- Cut 2 **medium squares** $2^7/_8$" x $2^7/_8$".

From gold print fabric:
- Cut 2 **large squares** $4^7/_8$" x $4^7/_8$".
- Cut 1 **center square** $4^1/_2$" x $4^1/_2$".

From blue print fabric:
- Cut 2 **large squares** $4^7/_8$" x $4^7/_8$".

From green print fabric:
- Cut 4 **small squares** $2^1/_2$" x $2^1/_2$".

From red print fabric:
- Cut 2 **small squares** $2^1/_2$" x $2^1/_2$".
- Cut 2 **medium squares** $2^7/_8$" x $2^7/_8$".

Use ¹/₄" seam allowances throughout.

1 Draw diagonal line (corner to corner) on wrong side of each cream **medium square**. With right sides together, place 1 cream **medium square** on top of 1 red **medium square**. Stitch seam ¹/₄" from each side of drawn line (**Fig. 1**).

2 Cut along drawn line and press open to make 2 **Small Triangle-Squares**. Make 4 **Small Triangle-Squares**.

3 Repeat Steps 1 and 2 using **large squares** to make 4 gold and blue **Large Triangle-Squares**.

4 Sew 2 **Small Triangle-Squares**, 1 red **small square**, and 1 cream **small square** together to make **Unit 1**. Make 2 **Unit 1's**.

5 Sew 2 green **small squares** and 2 cream **small squares** together to make **Unit 2**. Make 2 **Unit 2's**.

Fig. 1

Small Triangle-Squares
(make 4)

Large Triangle-Squares
(make 4)

Unit 1
(make 2)

Unit 2
(make 2)

DUBLIN STEPS

6 Sew 1 **Unit 1**, 1 **Large Triangle-Square**, and 1 **Unit 2** together to make **Unit 3**. Make 2 **Unit 3's**.

7 Sew 2 **Large Triangle-Squares** and **center square** together to make **Unit 4**.

8 Sew 2 **Unit 3's** and **Unit 4** together as shown in **Block Assembly** to complete **Block**.

Unit 3
(make 2)

Unit 4

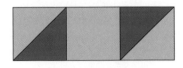

Block Assembly

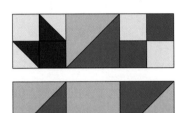

Block

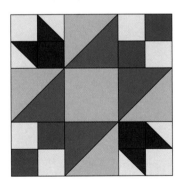

DUBLIN STEPS

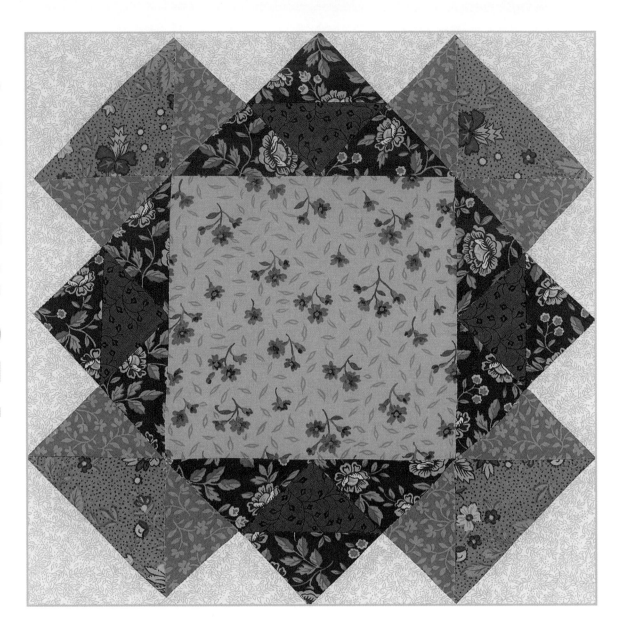

CUTTING OUT THE PIECES

From cream print fabric:
- Cut 2 **medium squares** $3^7/_8$" x $3^7/_8$".
- Cut 2 squares $4^1/_4$" x $4^1/_4$". Cut squares *twice* diagonally to make 8 **triangles**.

From green print fabric:
- Cut 2 squares $4^1/_4$" x $4^1/_4$". Cut squares *twice* diagonally to make 8 **triangles**.

From teal print fabric:
- Cut 2 **medium squares** $3^7/_8$" x $3^7/_8$".

From gold print fabric:
- Cut 1 **large square** $6^1/_2$" x $6^1/_2$".

From burgundy floral fabric:
- Cut 2 **small squares** 3" x 3".
- Cut 2 squares $4^1/_4$" x $4^1/_4$". Cut squares *twice* diagonally to make 8 **triangles**.

From burgundy print fabric:
- Cut 2 **small squares** 3" x 3".

72

Use ¹/₄" seam allowances throughout.

1 Draw diagonal line (corner to corner) on wrong side of each cream **medium square**. With right sides together, place 1 cream **medium square** on top of 1 teal **medium square**. Stitch seam ¹/₄" from each side of drawn line (**Fig. 1**).

2 Cut along drawn line and press open to make 2 **Large Triangle-Squares**. Make 4 **Large Triangle-Squares**.

3 Repeating Steps 1 and 2, use **small squares** to make 4 burgundy floral and burgundy print **Small Triangle-Squares**.

4 Sew 1 **Small Triangle-Square** and 2 burgundy floral **triangles** together to make **Unit 1**. Make 4 **Unit 1's**.

5 Sew 1 cream **triangle** and 1 green **triangle** together to make **Unit 2**. Make 4 **Unit 2a's** and 4 **Unit 2b's**.

6 Sew 1 **Unit 1**, 1 **Unit 2a**, and 1 **Unit 2b** together to make **Unit 3**. Make 4 **Unit 3's**.

Fig. 1

Large Triangle-Squares
(make 4)

Small Triangle-Squares
(make 4)

Unit 1
(make 4)

Unit 2a
(make 4)

Unit 2b
(make 4)

Unit 3
(make 4)

FLOWER POT

7 Sew 1 **Unit 3** and 2 **Large Triangle-Squares** together to make **Unit 4**. Make 2 **Unit 4's.**

8 Sew 2 **Unit 3's** and **large square** together to make **Unit 5.**

9 Sew 2 **Unit 4's** and **Unit 5** together as shown in **Block Assembly Diagram** to complete **Block.**

Unit 4
(make 2)

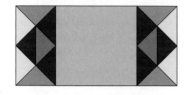

Unit 5

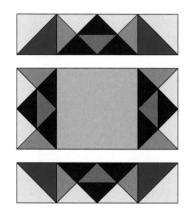

Block Assembly

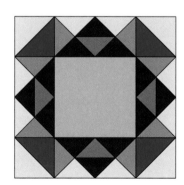

Block

74

FLOWER POT

CUTTING OUT THE PIECES

From tan and green print fabric:
- Cut 4 **large squares** $4^1/_2$" x $4^1/_2$".
- Cut 10 **small squares** $2^7/_8$" x $2^7/_8$".

From green print fabric:
- Cut 10 **small squares** $2^7/_8$" x $2^7/_8$".

Use ¹/₄" seam allowances throughout.

1 Draw diagonal line (corner to corner) on wrong side of each tan and green **small square**. With right sides together, place 1 tan and green **small square** on top of 1 green **small square**. Stitch seam ¹/₄" from each side of drawn line (**Fig. 1**).

2 Cut along drawn line and press open to make 2 **Triangle-Squares**. Make 20 **Triangle-Squares**.

3 Sew 4 **Triangle-Squares** together to make **Unit 1a**. Make 3 **Unit 1a's**. Sew 4 **Triangle-Squares** together to make **Unit 1b**. Make 2 **Unit 1b's**.

4 Sew 1 **Unit 1a**, 1 **Unit 1b**, and 1 **large square** together to make **Unit 2**. Make 2 **Unit 2's**.

Fig. 1

Triangle-Squares
(make 20)

Unit 1a
(make 3)

Unit 1b
(make 2)

Unit 2
(make 2)

5 Sew 1 **Unit 1a** and 2 **large squares** together to make **Unit 3**.

6 Sew 2 **Unit 2's** and **Unit 3** together as shown in **Block Assembly** to complete **Block**.

Unit 3

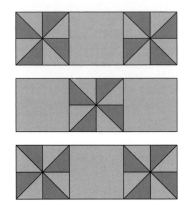

Block Assembly

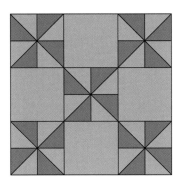

Block

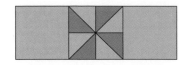

FLUTTER WHEEL

FLYING DUTCHMAN

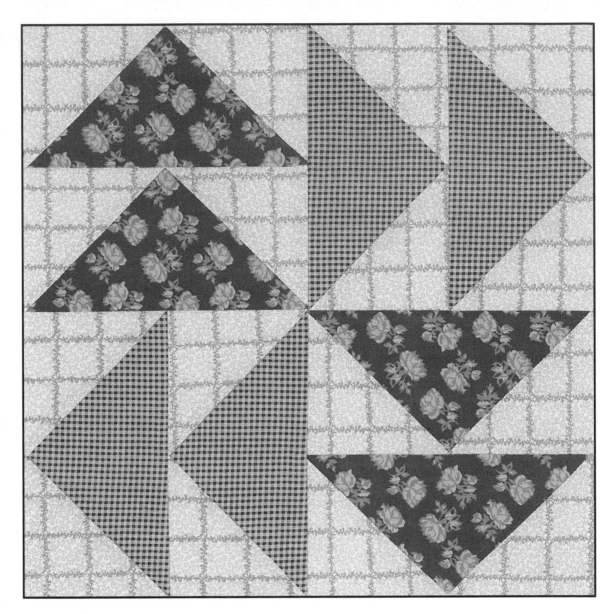

CUTTING OUT THE PIECES

From tan print fabric:
- Cut 16 **squares** $3^1/_2$" x $3^1/_2$".

From blue print fabric:
- Cut 4 **rectangles** $6^1/_2$" x $3^1/_2$".

From blue checked fabric:
- Cut 4 **rectangles** $6^1/_2$" x $3^1/_2$".

Use ¹/₄" seam allowances throughout.

1 With right sides together, place 1 **square** on 1 end of 1 blue print **rectangle** and stitch diagonally (**Fig. 1**). Trim ¹/₄" from stitching line (**Fig. 2**). Open up and press, pressing seam allowance to darker fabric (**Fig. 3**).

2 Place another **square** on opposite end of **rectangle**. Stitch and trim as shown in **Fig. 4**. Open up and press to complete **Flying Geese Unit A**. Make 4 **Flying Geese Unit A's**.

3 Repeat Steps 1 and 2 using tan **squares** and blue checked **rectangles** to make 4 **Flying Geese Unit B's**.

Fig. 1

Fig. 2

Fig. 3

Fig. 4

Flying Geese Unit A
(make 4)

Flying Geese Unit B
(make 4)

FLYING DUTCHMAN

4 Sew 2 **Flying Geese Unit A's** together to make **Unit 1**. Make 2 **Unit 1's**.

5 Sew 2 **Flying Geese Unit B's** together to make **Unit 2**. Make 2 **Unit 2's**.

6 Sew 2 **Unit 1's** and 2 **Unit 2's** together as shown in **Block Assembly** to complete **Block**.

Unit 1
(make 2)

Unit 2
(make 2)

Block Assembly

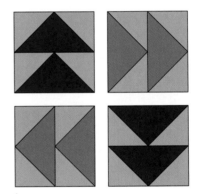

Block

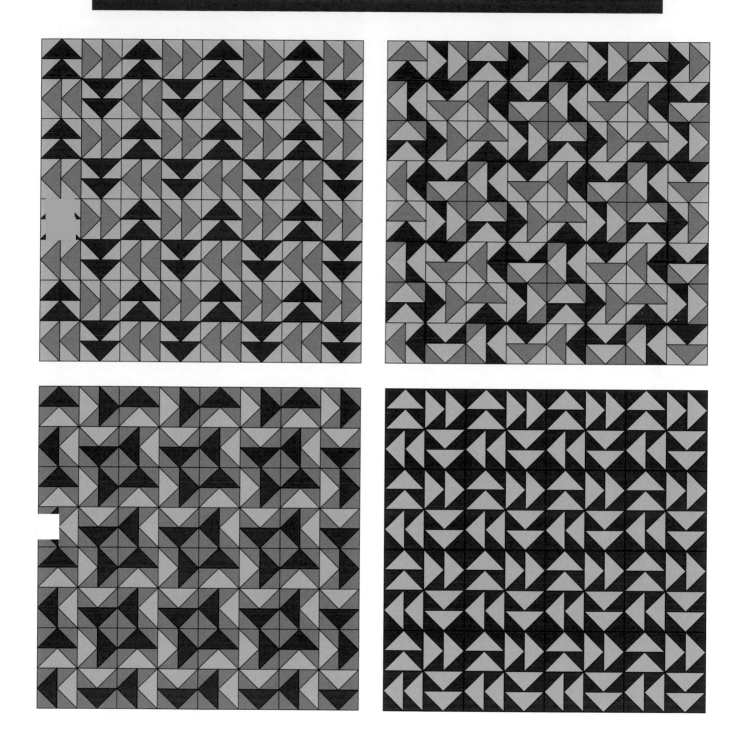

FLYING DUTCHMAN

FOX AND GEESE

CUTTING OUT THE PIECES

From tan print fabric:
- Cut 3 **large squares** $3^7/_8$" x $3^7/_8$".
- Cut 4 **small squares** $3^1/_2$" x $3^1/_2$".
- Cut 2 squares $3^7/_8$" x $3^7/_8$". Cut squares *once* diagonally to make 4 **small triangles**.

From orange print fabric:
- Cut 2 **large squares** $3^7/_8$" x $3^7/_8$".

From burgundy print fabric:
- Cut 1 **large square** $3^7/_8$" x $3^7/_8$".
- Cut 1 square $6^7/_8$" x $6^7/_8$". Cut square *once* diagonally to make 2 **large triangles**.

Use ¹/₄" seam allowances throughout.

1 Draw diagonal line (corner to corner) on wrong side of each tan **large square**. With right sides together, place 1 tan **large square** on top of 1 orange **large square**. Stitch seam ¹/₄" from each side of drawn line (**Fig. 1**).

2 Cut along drawn line and press open to make 2 **Triangle-Squares**. Repeat with remaining **large squares** to make a total of 4 tan and orange **Triangle-Squares** and 2 tan and burgundy **Triangle-Squares**.

3 Sew 1 tan and burgundy **Triangle-Square** and 2 **small triangles** together to make **Unit 1**. Make 2 **Unit 1's**.

4 Sew 1 **Unit 1** and 1 **large triangle** together to make **Unit 2**. Make 2 **Unit 2's**.

Fig. 1

Triangle-Squares

(make 4)

(make 2)

Unit 1
(make 2)

Unit 2
(make 2)

FOX AND GEESE

5 Sew 2 tan and orange **Triangle-Squares** and 2 **small squares** together to make **Unit 3**. Make 2 **Unit 3's**.

6 Sew 2 **Unit 2's** and 2 **Unit 3's** together as shown in **Block Assembly** to complete **Block**.

Unit 3
(make 2)

Block Assembly

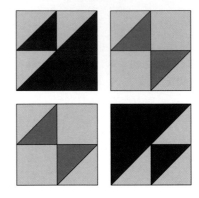

Block

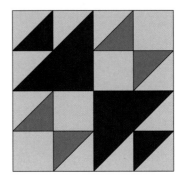

FOX AND GEESE

GENTLEMAN'S FANCY

CUTTING OUT THE PIECES

From cream print fabric:
- Cut 8 **small squares** $2^1/2$" x $2^1/2$".
- Cut 4 squares $2^7/8$" x $2^7/8$". Cut squares *once* diagonally to make 8 **small triangles**.
- Cut 4 **rectangles** $4^1/2$" x $2^1/2$".

From tan print fabric:
- Cut 1 **large square** $4^1/2$" x $4^1/2$".
- Cut 2 squares $4^7/8$" x $4^7/8$". Cut squares *once* diagonally to make 4 **large triangles**.

From burgundy print fabric:
- Cut 12 **small squares** $2^1/2$" x $2^1/2$".
- Cut 4 **rectangles** $4^1/2$" x $2^1/2$".

Use ¹/₄" seam allowances throughout.

1 With right sides together, place 1 cream **small square** on 1 end of 1 burgundy **rectangle** and stitch diagonally (**Fig. 1**). Trim ¹/₄" from stitching line (**Fig. 2**). Open up and press, pressing seam allowance to darker fabric (**Fig. 3**).

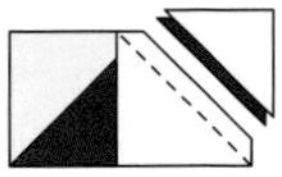

2 Place another cream **small square** on opposite end of **rectangle**. Stitch and trim as shown in **Fig. 4**. Open up and press to complete **Flying Geese Unit A**. Make 4 **Flying Geese Unit A's**.

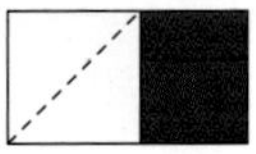

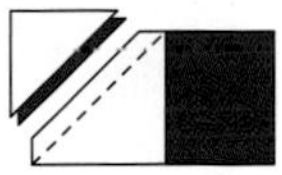

3 Using burgundy **small squares** and cream **rectangles**, repeat Steps 1 and 2 to make 4 **Flying Geese Unit B's**.

4 Sew 1 **Flying Geese Unit A** and 1 **Flying Geese Unit B** together to make **Unit 1**. Make 4 **Unit 1's**.

5 Sew 1 burgundy **small square** and 2 **small triangles** together to make **Unit 2**. Make 4 **Unit 2's**.

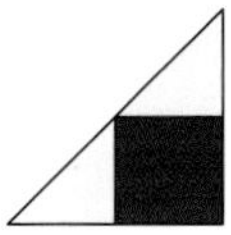

6 Sew 1 **Unit 2** and 1 **large triangle** together to make **Unit 3**. Make 4 **Unit 3's**.

Fig. 1

Fig. 2

Fig. 3

Fig. 4

Flying Geese Unit A
(make 4)

Flying Geese Unit B
(make 4)

Unit 1
(make 4)

Unit 2
(make 4)

Unit 3
(make 4)

GENTLEMAN'S FANCY

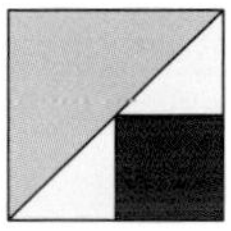

7 Sew 1 **Unit 1** and 2 **Unit 3's** together to make **Unit 4**. Make 2 **Unit 4's**.

8 Sew 2 **Unit 1's** and **large square** together to make **Unit 5**.

9 Sew 2 **Unit 4's** and **Unit 5** together as shown in **Block Assembly** to complete **Block**.

Unit 4
(make 2)

Unit 5

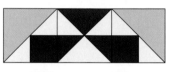

Block Assembly

Block

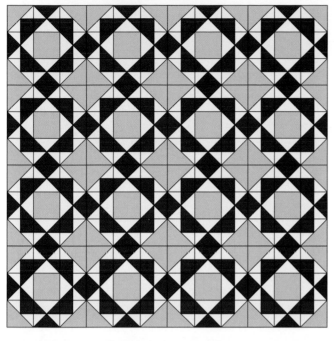

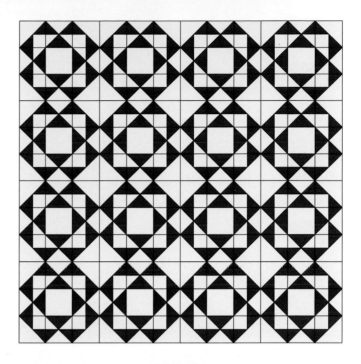

GENTLEMAN'S FANCY

GOLGOTHA

CUTTING OUT THE PIECES

From cream print fabric:
- Cut 2 **large squares** $3^1/4$" x $3^1/4$".
- Cut 4 **small squares** $2^1/2$" x $2^1/2$".
- Cut 8 **rectangles** $4^1/2$" x $2^1/2$".

From pink print fabric:
- Cut 1 **center square** $4^1/2$" x $4^1/2$".

From blue print fabric:
- Cut 16 **small squares** $2^1/2$" x $2^1/2$".

From burgundy print fabric:
- Cut 2 **large squares** $3^1/4$" x $3^1/4$".
- Cut 4 **medium squares** $2^7/8$" x $2^7/8$".

Use ¹/₄" seam allowances throughout.

1 With right sides together, place 1 blue **small square** on 1 end of 1 **rectangle** and stitch diagonally (**Fig. 1**). Trim ¹/₄" from stitching line (**Fig. 2**). Open up and press, pressing seam allowance to darker fabric (**Fig. 3**).

2 Place another blue **small square** on opposite end of **rectangle**. Stitch and trim as shown in **Fig. 4**. Open up and press to complete **Flying Geese Unit**. Make 4 **Flying Geese Units**.

3 With right sides together, place 1 blue **small square** on 1 corner of **center square** and stitch diagonally (**Fig. 5**). Trim ¹/₄" from stitching line (**Fig. 6**). Open up and press, pressing seam allowance to darker fabric (**Fig. 7**).

4 Continue adding blue **small squares** to corners of **center square** as shown in **Fig. 8**. Open up and press to complete **Unit 1**.

5 Draw diagonal lines from corner to corner in both directions on wrong side of each cream **large square**. With right sides together, place 1 cream **large square** on top of 1 burgundy **large square**. Stitch seam ¹/₄" from each side of 1 drawn line (**Fig. 9**). Press stitching. Cut apart along drawn line to make 2 **Triangle-Squares**. Make 4 **Triangles-Squares**.

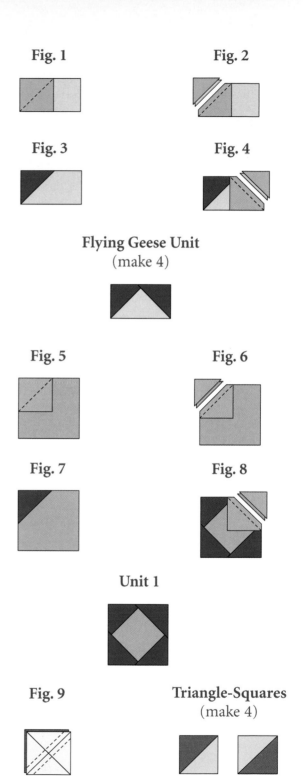

Fig. 1

Fig. 2

Fig. 3

Fig. 4

Flying Geese Unit
(make 4)

Fig. 5

Fig. 6

Fig. 7

Fig. 8

Unit 1

Fig. 9

Triangle-Squares
(make 4)

GOLGOTHA

6 On wrong side of **Triangle-Squares**, extend drawn line from corner of cream triangle to corner of burgundy triangle.

7 With right sides together, place 1 **Triangle-Square** on top of 1 burgundy **medium square**. Stitch seam ¼" on each side of drawn line (**Fig. 10**). Cut apart along drawn line (**Fig. 11**) to make 1 **Unit 2a** and 1 **Unit 2b**; press units open. Make 4 *each* of **Unit 2a** and **Unit 2b**.

8 Sew 1 **Unit 2a**, 1 **Unit 2b**, 1 cream **small square**, and 1 blue **small square** together to make **Unit 3**. Make 4 **Unit 3's**.

9 Sew 1 **Flying Geese Unit** and 1 **rectangle** together to make **Unit 4**. Make 4 **Unit 4's**.

10 Sew 2 **Unit 3's** and 1 **Unit 4** together to make **Unit 5**. Make 2 **Unit 5's**.

11 Sew 2 **Unit 4's** and **Unit 1** together to make **Unit 6**.

12 Sew 2 **Unit 5's** and **Unit 6** together as shown in **Block Assembly** to complete **Block**.

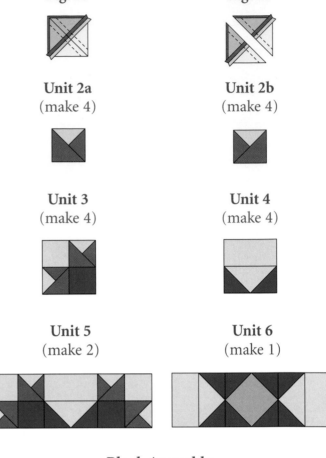

Fig. 10   Fig. 11

Unit 2a   Unit 2b
(make 4)   (make 4)

Unit 3   Unit 4
(make 4)   (make 4)

Unit 5   Unit 6
(make 2)   (make 1)

Block Assembly

Block

94

95

GOLGOTHA

HEN AND CHICKS

CUTTING OUT THE PIECES

From cream print fabric:
- Cut 6 **medium squares** $2^7/_8$" x $2^7/_8$".
- Cut 12 **small squares** $2^1/_2$" x $2^1/_2$".
- Cut 2 squares $4^7/_8$" x $4^7/_8$". Cut squares *once* diagonally to make 4 **large triangles**.
- Cut 4 squares $2^7/_8$" x $2^7/_8$". Cut squares *once* diagonally to make 8 **small triangles**.

From blue print fabric:
- Cut 2 **medium squares** $2^7/_8$" x $2^7/_8$".
- Cut 4 **rectangles** $4^1/_2$" x $2^1/_2$".

From red print fabric:
- Cut 4 **medium squares** $2^7/_8$" x $2^7/_8$".

Use ¼" seam allowances throughout.

1 Draw diagonal line (corner to corner) on wrong side of each cream **medium square**. With right sides together, place 1 cream **medium square** on top of 1 blue **medium square**. Stitch seam ¼" from each side of drawn line (**Fig. 1**).

Fig. 1

Triangle-Squares

(make 4)   (make 8)

2 Cut along drawn line and press open to make 2 **Triangle-Squares**. Make 4 blue and cream **Triangle-Squares** and 8 red and cream **Triangle-Squares**.

Fig. 2   **Fig. 3**

3 With right sides together, place 1 cream **small square** on 1 end of 1 **rectangle** and stitch diagonally (**Fig. 2**). Trim ¼" from stitching line (**Fig. 3**). Open up and press, pressing seam allowance to darker fabric (**Fig. 4**).

Fig. 4   **Fig. 5**

Flying Geese Unit
(make 4)

4 Place another cream **small square** on opposite end of **rectangle**. Stitch and trim as shown in **Fig. 5**. Open up and press to complete **Flying Geese Unit**. Make 4 **Flying Geese Units**.

Unit 1
(make 4)

5 Sew 1 **Flying Geese Unit** and 2 red and cream **Triangle-Squares** together to make **Unit 1**. Make 4 **Unit 1's**.

HEN AND CHICKS

6 Sew 1 **Unit 1** and 2 cream **small squares** together to make **Unit 2**. Make 2 **Unit 2's**.

7 Sew 1 blue and cream **Triangle-Square** and 2 **small triangles** together to make **Unit 3**. Make 4 **Unit 3's**.

8 Sew 1 **Unit 3** and 1 **large triangle** together to make **Unit 4**. Make 4 **Unit 4's**.

9 Sew 4 **Unit 4's** together to make **Unit 5**.

10 Sew **Unit 5** and 2 **Unit 1's** together to make **Unit 6**.

11 Sew **Unit 6** and 2 **Unit 2's** together as shown in **Block Assembly** to complete **Block**.

Unit 2
(make 2)

Unit 3
(make 4)

Unit 4
(make 4)

Unit 5   **Unit 6**

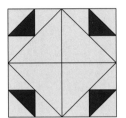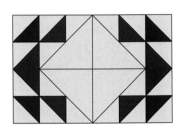

Block Assembly

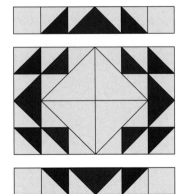

Block

HEN AND CHICKS

JACOB'S LADDER

From cream print fabric:
- Cut 24 **small squares** 2" x 2".

From burgundy checked fabric:
- Cut 12 **rectangles** $3^1/_2$" x 2".

From dark burgundy print fabric:
- Cut 1 **medium square** $3^1/_2$" x $3^1/_2$".

From gold print fabric:
- Cut 4 **large squares** 5" x 5".

Use ¼" seam allowances throughout.

1 With right sides together, place 1 **small square** on 1 end of 1 **rectangle** and stitch diagonally (**Fig. 1**). Trim ¼" from stitching line (**Fig. 2**). Open up and press, pressing seam allowance to darker fabric (**Fig. 3**).

2 Place another **small square** on opposite end of **rectangle**. Stitch and trim as shown in **Fig. 4**. Open up and press to complete **Flying Geese Unit**. Make 12 **Flying Geese Units**.

3 Sew 3 **Flying Geese Units** together to make **Unit 1**. Make 4 **Unit 1's**.

4 Sew 1 **Unit 1** and 2 **large squares** together to make **Unit 2**. Make 2 **Unit 2's**.

Fig. 1

Fig. 2

Fig. 3

Fig. 4

Flying Geese Unit
(make 12)

Unit 1

Unit 2

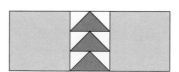

JACOB'S LADDER

5 Sew 2 **Unit 1's** and **medium square** together to make **Unit 3**.

6 Sew 2 **Unit 2's** and **Unit 3** together as shown in **Block Assembly** to complete **Block**.

Block Assembly

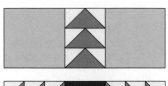

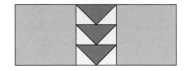

Block

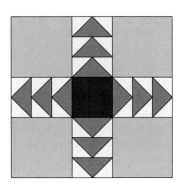

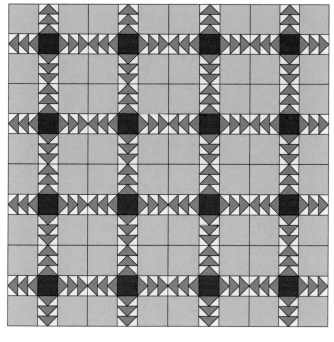
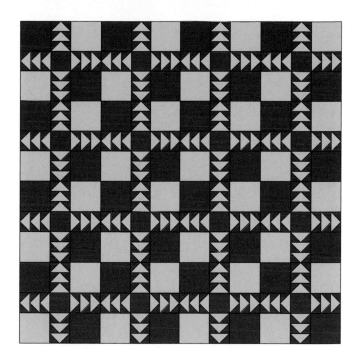

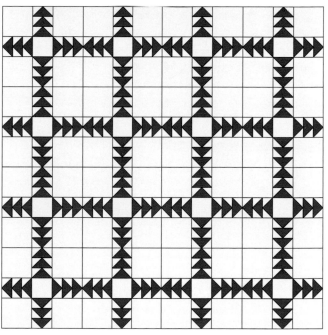

CUTTING OUT THE PIECES

From cream print fabric:
- Cut 8 **large squares** $2^3/8$" x $2^3/8$".
- Cut 4 **small squares** 2" x 2".

From brown print fabric:
- Cut 8 **large squares** $2^3/8$" x $2^3/8$".
- Cut 4 squares $2^3/8$" x $2^3/8$". Cut squares *once* diagonally to make 8 **small triangles**.

From teal print fabric:
- Cut 2 squares $3^7/8$" x $3^7/8$". Cut squares *once* diagonally to make 4 **medium triangles**.

From gold print fabric:
- Cut 2 squares $6^7/8$" x $6^7/8$". Cut squares *once* diagonally to make 4 **large triangles**.

Use ¹/₄" seam allowances throughout.

1 Draw diagonal line (corner to corner) on wrong side of each cream **large square**. With right sides together, place 1 cream **large square** on top of 1 brown **large square**. Stitch seam ¹/₄" from each side of drawn line (**Fig. 1**).

Fig. 1

Triangle-Squares
(make 16)

2 Cut along drawn line and press open to make 2 **Triangle-Squares**. Make 16 **Triangle-Squares**.

Unit 1
(make 8)

3 Sew 2 **Triangle-Squares** and 1 **small triangle** together to make **Unit 1**. Make 8 **Unit 1's**.

Unit 2
(make 4)

4 Sew 1 **Unit 1** and 1 **small square** together to make **Unit 2**. Make 4 **Unit 2's**.

Unit 3
(make 4)

5 Sew 1 **Unit 1** and 1 **medium triangle** together to make **Unit 3**. Make 4 **Unit 3's**.

KANSAS TROUBLES

6 Sew 1 **Unit 2** and 1 **Unit 3** together to make **Unit 4**. Make 4 **Unit 4's**.

7 Sew 1 **Unit 4** and 1 **large triangle** together to make **Unit 5**. Make 4 **Unit 5's**.

8 Sew 4 **Unit 5's** together as shown in **Block Assembly** to complete **Block**.

Unit 4
(make 4)

Unit 5
(make 4)

Block Assembly

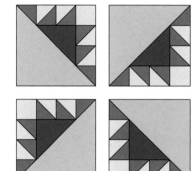

Block

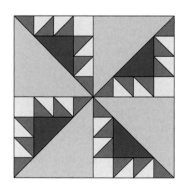

KANSAS TROUBLES

CUTTING OUT THE PIECES

From tan print fabric:
- Cut 1 **large square** $4^1/2$" x $4^1/2$".
- Cut 4 **medium squares** $2^7/8$" x $2^7/8$".
- Cut 12 **small squares** $2^1/2$" x $2^1/2$".
- Cut 4 **rectangles** $4^1/2$" x $2^1/2$".

From light green print fabric:
- Cut 4 **medium squares** $2^7/8$" x $2^7/8$".
- Cut 4 **small squares** $2^1/2$" x $2^1/2$". `

From dark green print fabric:
- Cut 8 **small squares** $2^1/2$" x $2^1/2$".
- Cut 4 **rectangles** $4^1/2$" x $2^1/2$".

Use ¹/₄" seam allowances throughout.

1 Draw diagonal line (corner to corner) on wrong side of each tan **medium square**. With right sides together, place 1 tan **medium square** on top of 1 light green **medium square**. Stitch seam ¹/₄" from each side of drawn line (**Fig. 1**).

2 Cut along drawn line and press open to make 2 **Triangle-Squares**. Make 8 **Triangle-Squares**.

3 Sew 2 **Triangle-Squares**, 1 tan **small square**, and 1 light green **small square** together to make **Unit 1**. Make 4 **Unit 1's**.

4 With right sides together, place 1 tan **small square** on 1 end of 1 dark green **rectangle** and stitch diagonally (**Fig. 2**). Trim ¹/₄" from stitching line (**Fig. 3**). Open up and press, pressing seam allowance to darker fabric (**Fig. 4**).

5 Place another tan **small square** on opposite end of **rectangle**. Stitch and trim as shown in **Fig. 5**. Open up and press to complete **Flying Geese Unit A**. Make 4 **Flying Geese Unit A's**.

Fig. 1

Triangle-Squares
(make 8)

Unit 1
(make 4)

Fig. 2

Fig. 3

Fig. 4

Fig. 5

Flying Geese Unit A
(make 4)

LAUREL WREATH

6 Using dark green **small squares** and tan **rectangles**, repeat Steps 4 and 5 to make 4 **Flying Geese Unit B's.**

7 Sew 1 **Flying Geese Unit A** and 1 **Flying Geese Unit B** together to make **Unit 2**. Make 4 **Unit 2's.**

8 Sew 2 **Unit 1's** and 1 **Unit 2** together to make **Unit 3**. Make 2 **Unit 3's.**

9 Sew 2 **Unit 2's** and **large square** together to make **Unit 4.**

10 Sew 2 **Unit 3's** and **Unit 4** together as shown in **Block Assembly** to complete **Block.**

Flying Geese Unit B
(make 4)

Unit 2
(make 4)

Unit 3
(make 2)

Unit 4

Block Assembly

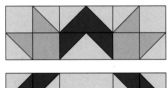

Block

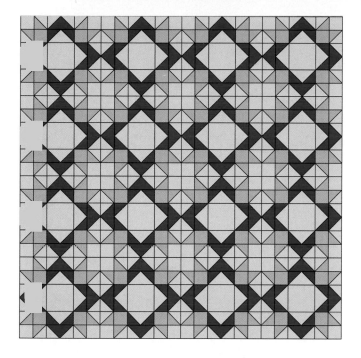

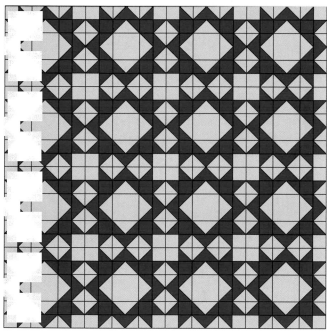

LAUREL WREATH

LONDON ROADS

CUTTING OUT THE PIECES

From cream print fabric:
- Cut 2 **large squares** $5^1/4$" x $5^1/4$".
- Cut 1 **small square** $4^1/2$" x $4^1/2$".
- Cut 4 **large rectangles** $4^1/2$" x 2".

From burgundy print fabric:
- Cut 2 **large squares** $5^1/4$" x $5^1/4$".

From teal print fabric:
- Cut 8 **small rectangles** $4^1/2$" x $1^3/4$".

Use ¹/₄" seam allowances throughout.

1 Draw diagonal lines from corner to corner in both directions on wrong side of each cream **large square**. With right sides together, place 1 cream **large square** on top of 1 burgundy **large square**. Stitch seam ¹/₄" from each side of 1 drawn line (**Fig. 1**). Press stitching. Cut apart along drawn line (**Fig. 2**) to make 2 **Triangle-Squares**. Make 4 **Triangle-Squares**.

2 On wrong side of 2 **Triangle-Squares**, extend drawn line from corner of cream triangle to corner of burgundy triangle.

3 Match 1 marked **Triangle-Square** and 1 unmarked **Triangle-Square** with contrasting fabrics facing and marked unit on top. Stitch seam ¹/₄" on each side of drawn line (**Fig. 3**). Cut apart along drawn line (**Fig. 4**) to make 2 **Hourglass Units**; press **Hourglass Units** open. Make 4 **Hourglass Units**.

Fig. 1

Fig. 2

Triangle-Squares
(make 4)

Fig. 3

Fig. 4

Hourglass Units
(make 4)

113

4 Sew 2 **small rectangles** and 1 **large rectangle** together to make **Unit 1**. Make 4 **Unit 1's**.

5 Sew 2 **Hourglass Units** and 1 **Unit 1** together to make **Unit 2**. Make 2 **Unit 2's**.

6 Sew 2 **Unit 1's** and **small square** together to make **Unit 3**.

7 Sew 2 **Unit 2's** and **Unit 3** together as shown in **Block Assembly** to complete **Block**.

Unit 1
(make 4)

Unit 2
(make 2)

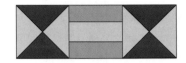

Unit 3

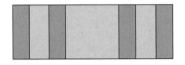

Block Assembly

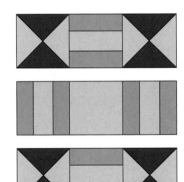

Block

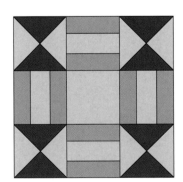

115

LONDON ROADS

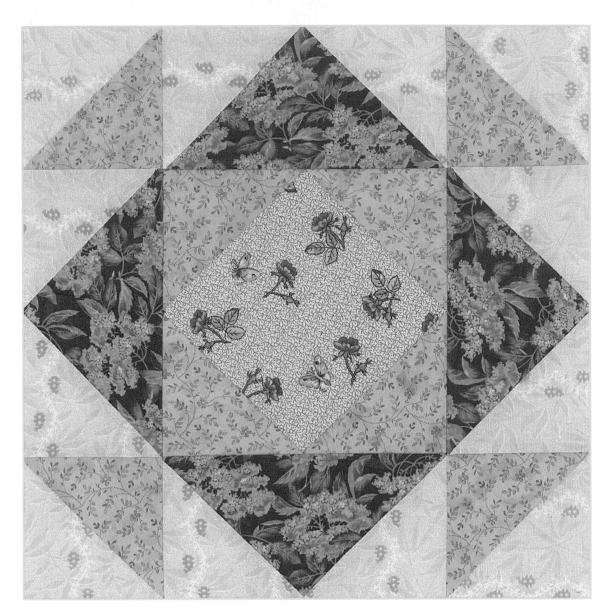

CUTTING OUT THE PIECES

From cream print fabric:
- Cut 2 **medium squares** $3^7/_8$" x $3^7/_8$".
- Cut 8 **small squares** $3^1/_2$" x $3^1/_2$".

From light green print fabric:
- Cut 2 **medium squares** $3^7/_8$" x $3^7/_8$".
- Cut 4 **small squares** $3^1/_2$" x $3^1/_2$".

From dark green print fabric:
- Cut 4 **rectangles** $6^1/_2$" x $3^1/_2$".

From gold print fabric:
- Cut 1 **large square** $6^1/_2$" x $6^1/_2$".

Use ¼" seam allowances throughout.

1 Draw diagonal line (corner to corner) on wrong side of each cream **medium square**. With right sides together, place 1 cream **medium square** on top of 1 light green **medium square**. Stitch seam ¼" from each side of drawn line (**Fig. 1**).

Fig. 1   Triangle-squares
           (make 4)

2 Cut along drawn line and press open to make 2 **Triangle-Squares**. Make 4 **Triangle-Squares**.

Fig. 2   Fig. 3

3 With right sides together, place 1 cream **small square** on 1 end of 1 **rectangle** and stitch diagonally (**Fig. 2**). Trim ¼" from stitching line (**Fig. 3**). Open up and press, pressing seam allowance to darker fabric (**Fig. 4**).

Fig. 4   Fig. 5

Flying Geese Unit
(make 4)

4 Place another cream **small square** on opposite end of **rectangle**. Stitch and trim as shown in **Fig. 5**. Open up and press to complete **Flying Geese Unit**. Make 4 **Flying Geese Units**.

Fig. 6   Fig. 7

5 With right sides together, place 1 light green **small square** on 1 corner of **large square** and stitch diagonally (**Fig. 6**). Trim ¼" from stitching line (**Fig. 7**). Open up and press, pressing seam allowance to darker fabric (**Fig. 8**).

Fig. 8

6 Continue adding light green **small squares** to corners of **large square** as shown in **Fig. 9**. Open up and press to complete **Unit 1**.

Fig. 9

7 Sew 2 **Triangle-Squares** and 1 **Flying Geese Unit** together to make **Unit 2**. Make 2 **Unit 2's**.

Unit 2
(make 2)

8 Sew **Unit 1** and 2 **Flying Geese Units** together to make **Unit 3**.

Unit 3

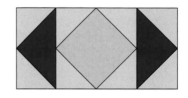

9 Sew 2 **Unit 2's** and **Unit 3** together as shown in **Block Assembly** to complete **Block**.

Block Assembly

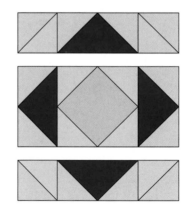

Block

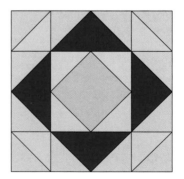

MAPLE LEAF

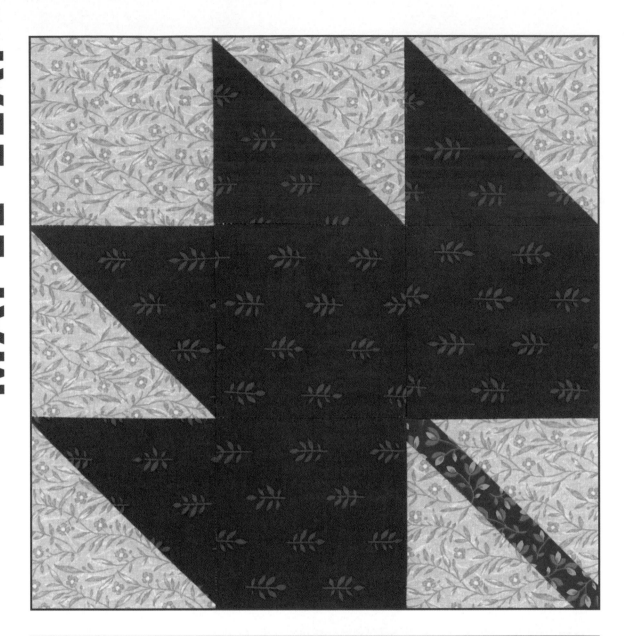

CUTTING OUT THE PIECES

From tan print fabric:
- Cut 2 **large squares** $4^7/_8$" x $4^7/_8$".
- Cut 1 **medium square** $4^1/_2$" x $4^1/_2$".
- Cut 2 **small squares** 4" x 4".

From brown print fabric:
- Cut 2 **large squares** $4^7/_8$" x $4^7/_8$".
- Cut 3 **medium squares** $4^1/_2$" x $4^1/_2$".

From green print fabric:
- Cut 1 **medium square** $4^1/_2$" x $4^1/_2$".

Use ¹/₄" seam allowances throughout.

1 Draw diagonal line (corner to corner) on wrong side of each tan **large square**. With right sides together, place 1 tan **large square** on top of 1 brown **large square**. Stitch seam ¹/₄" from each side of drawn line (**Fig. 1**).

2 Cut along drawn line and press open to make 2 **Triangle-Squares**. Make 4 **Triangle-Squares**.

3 With right sides together, place 1 **small square** on 1 corner of green **medium square** and stitch diagonally (**Fig. 2**). Trim ¹/₄" from stitching line (**Fig. 3**). Open up and press, pressing seam allowance to darker fabric (**Fig. 4**).

4 Add 1 **small square** to opposite corner of **medium square** as shown in **Fig. 5**. Open up and press to complete **Unit 1**.

Fig. 1

Triangle-Squares
(make 4)

Fig. 2

Fig. 3

Fig. 4

Fig. 5

Unit 1

MAPLE LEAF

5 Sew tan **medium square** and 2 **Triangle-Squares** together to make **Unit 2.**

6 Sew 1 **Triangle-Square** and 2 brown **medium squares** together to make **Unit 3.**

7 Sew 1 **Triangle-Square**, 1 brown **medium square**, and **Unit 1** together to make **Unit 4.**

8 Sew **Unit 2, Unit 3,** and **Unit 4** together as shown in **Block Assembly** to complete **Block.**

Unit 2

Unit 3

Unit 4

Block Assembly

Block

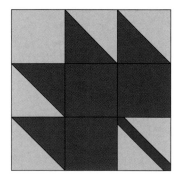

MAPLE LEAF

CUTTING OUT THE PIECES

From cream print fabric:
- Cut 4 **medium squares** $2^7/_8$" x $2^7/_8$".
- Cut 4 **small squares** $2^1/_2$" x $2^1/_2$".
- Cut 4 **rectangles** $4^1/_2$" x $2^1/_2$".

From burgundy print fabric:
- Cut 1 **large square** $4^1/_2$" x $4^1/_2$".
- Cut 8 **small squares** $2^1/_2$" x $2^1/_2$".
- Cut 4 **rectangles** $4^1/_2$" x $2^1/_2$".

From teal print fabric:
- Cut 4 **medium squares** $2^7/_8$" x $2^7/_8$".
- Cut 8 **small squares** $2^1/_2$" x $2^1/_2$".

From gold print fabric:
- Cut 4 **small squares** $2^1/_2$" x $2^1/_2$".

Use ¹/₄" seam allowances throughout.

1 Draw diagonal line (corner to corner) on wrong side of each cream **medium square**. With right sides together, place 1 cream **medium square** on top of 1 teal **medium square**. Stitch seam ¹/₄" from each side of drawn line (**Fig. 1**).

2 Cut along drawn line and press open to make 2 **Triangle-Squares**. Make 8 **Triangle-Squares**.

3 Sew 2 **Triangle-Squares**, 1 cream **small square**, and 1 gold **small square** together to make **Unit 1**. Make 4 **Unit 1's**.

4 With right sides together, place 1 burgundy **small square** on 1 end of 1 cream **rectangle** and stitch diagonally (**Fig. 2**). Trim ¹/₄" from stitching line (**Fig. 3**). Open up and press, pressing seam allowance to darker fabric (**Fig. 4**).

5 Place another burgundy **small square** on opposite end of **rectangle**. Stitch and trim as shown in **Fig. 5**. Open up and press to complete **Flying Geese Unit A**. Make 4 **Flying Geese Units A's**.

Fig. 1

Triangle-Squares
(make 8)

Unit 1
(make 4)

Fig. 2

Fig. 3

Fig. 4

Fig. 5

Flying Geese Unit A
(make 4)

MEMORY

6 Repeat Steps 3 and 4 using teal **small squares** and burgundy **rectangles** to make 4 **Flying Geese Units B.** Make 4 **Flying Geese Units B's.**

7 Sew 1 **Flying Geese Unit A** and 1 **Flying Geese Unit B** together to make **Unit 2.** Make 4 **Unit 2's.**

8 Sew 2 **Unit 1's** and 1 **Unit 2** together to make **Unit 3.** Make 2 **Unit 3's.**

9 Sew 2 **Unit 2's** and **large square** together to make **Unit 4.**

10 Sew 2 **Unit 3's** and **Unit 4** together as shown in **Block Assembly** to complete **Block.**

Flying Geese Unit B
(make 4)

Unit 2
(make 4)

Unit 3
(make 2)

Unit 4

Block Assembly

Block

MEMORY

CUTTING OUT THE PIECES

From cream print fabric:
- Cut 1 **large square** $4^1/_2"$ x $4^1/_2"$.
- Cut 28 **small squares** $2^1/_2"$ x $2^1/_2"$.

From light blue print fabric:
- Cut 4 **small squares** $2^1/_2"$ x $2^1/_2"$.

From dark blue print fabric:
- Cut 8 **rectangles** $4^1/_2"$ x $2^1/_2"$.

Use ¹/₄" seam allowances throughout.

1 With right sides together, place 1 cream **small square** on 1 end of 1 **rectangle** and stitch diagonally (**Fig. 1**). Trim ¹/₄" from stitching line (**Fig. 2**). Open up and press, pressing seam allowance to darker fabric (**Fig. 3**).

2 Place another cream **small square** on opposite end of **rectangle**. Stitch and trim as shown in **Fig. 4**. Open up and press to complete **Flying Geese Unit**. Make 8 **Flying Geese Units**.

3 Sew 2 **Flying Geese Units** together to make **Unit 1**. Make 4 **Unit 1's**.

4 Sew 1 light blue **small square** and 3 cream **small squares** together to make **Unit 2**. Make 4 **Unit 2's**.

Fig. 1

Fig. 2

Fig. 3

Fig. 4

Flying Geese Unit
(make 8)

Unit 1
(make 4)

Unit 2
(make 4)

MRS. BRYAN'S CHOICE

5 Sew 1 **Unit 1** and 2 **Unit 2's** together to make **Unit 3**. Make 2 **Unit 3's**.

6 Sew 2 **Unit 1's** and **large square** together to make **Unit 4**.

7 Sew 2 **Unit 3's** and **Unit 4** together as shown in **Block Assembly** to complete **Block**.

Unit 3
(make 2)

Unit 4

Block Assembly

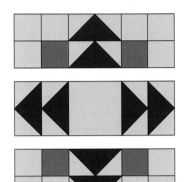

Block

MRS. BRYAN'S CHOICE

CUTTING OUT THE PIECES

From cream print fabric:
- Cut 1 **large square** $6^7/_8$"x $6^7/_8$".
- Cut 6 **small squares** 3" x 3".
- Cut 2 squares $5^3/_8$" x $5^3/_8$". Cut squares *once* diagonally to make 4 **large triangles**.
- Cut 1 square $4^1/_4$" x $4^1/_4$". Cut square *twice* diagonally to make 4 **small triangles**. (You will use 2 and have 2 left over.)

From blue fabric:
- Cut 6 **small squares** 3" x 3".
- Cut 1 square $4^1/_4$" x $4^1/_4$". Cut square *twice* diagonally to make 4 **small triangles**. (You will use 2 and have 2 left over.)

Use ¼" seam allowances throughout.

1 Draw diagonal line (corner to corner) on wrong side of each cream **small square**. With right sides together, place 1 cream **small square** on top of 1 blue **small square**. Stitch seam ¼" from each side of drawn line (**Fig. 1**).

Fig. 1

Triangle-Squares
(make 12)

2 Cut along drawn line and press open to make 2 **Triangle-Squares**. Make 12 **Triangle-Squares**.

Unit 1
(make 2)

3 Sew 3 **Triangle-Squares** together to make **Unit 1**. Make 2 **Unit 1's**.

Unit 2
(make 2)

4 Sew 1 cream **small triangle**, 1 **Unit 1**, and 1 blue **small triangle** together to make **Unit 2**. Make 2 **Unit 2's**.

Unit 3
(make 2)

5 Sew 3 **Triangle-Squares** together to make **Unit 3**. Make 2 **Unit 3's**.

NAVAJO

6 Sew 2 **Unit 3's**, 2 **large triangles**, and **large square** together to make **Unit 4**.

7 Sew 2 **large triangles**, 2 **Unit 2's**, and **Unit 4** together as shown in **Block Assembly** to complete **Block**.

Unit 4

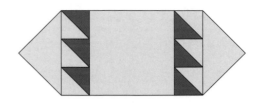

Block Assembly

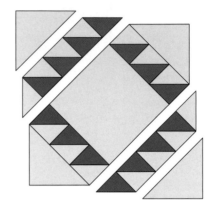

Block

NAVAJO

NINE-PATCH STAR

CUTTING OUT THE PIECES

From cream print fabric:
- Cut 4 **large squares** $4^7/_8$" x $4^7/_8$".
- Cut 1 **small square** $4^1/_2$" x $4^1/_2$".

From gold print fabric:
- Cut 2 **large squares** $4^7/_8$" x $4^7/_8$".

From red print fabric:
- Cut 2 **large squares** $4^7/_8$" x $4^7/_8$".

Use ¹/₄" seam allowances throughout.

1 Draw diagonal line (corner to corner) on wrong side of each cream **large square**. With right sides together, place 1 cream **large square** on top of 1 gold **large square**. Stitch seam ¹/₄" from each side of drawn line (**Fig. 1**).

Fig. 1

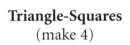

Triangle-Squares
(make 4)

2 Cut along drawn line and press open to make 2 **Triangle-Squares**. Repeat to make 4 cream and gold **Triangle-Squares** and 4 cream and red **Triangle-Squares**.

(make 4)

3 Sew 2 cream and gold **Triangle-Squares** and 1 cream and red **Triangle-Square** together to make **Unit 1**. Make 2 **Unit 1's**.

Unit 1
(make 2)

NINE-PATCH STAR

4 Sew 2 cream and red **Triangle-Squares** and **small square** together to make **Unit 2**.

Unit 2

5 Sew 2 **Unit 1's** and **Unit 2** together as shown in **Block Assembly** to complete **Block**.

Block Assembly

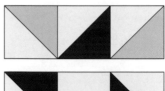

Block

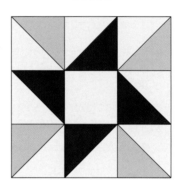

NINE-PATCH STAR

CUTTING OUT THE PIECES

From cream print fabric:
- Cut 1 **large square** $6^1/_2$" x $6^1/_2$".
- Cut 48 **small squares** 2" x 2".

From burgundy print fabric:
- Cut 24 **rectangles** $3^1/_2$" x 2".

ASSEMBLING THE BLOCK

Use ¹/₄" seam allowances throughout.

1 With right sides together, place 1 **small square** on 1 end of 1 **rectangle** and stitch diagonally (**Fig. 1**). Trim ¹/₄" from stitching line (**Fig. 2**). Open up and press, pressing seam allowance to darker fabric (**Fig. 3**).

2 Place another **small square** on opposite end of **rectangle**. Stitch and trim as shown in **Fig. 4**. Open up and press to complete **Flying Geese Unit**. Make 24 **Flying Geese Units**.

3 Sew 2 **Flying Geese Units** together to make **Unit 1**. Make 2 **Unit 1's**.

4 Sew 3 **Flying Geese Units** together to make **Unit 2**. Make 4 **Unit 2's**.

5 Sew 4 **Flying Geese Units** together to make **Unit 3**. Make 2 **Unit 3's**.

6 Sew **large square** and 2 **Unit 1's** together to make **Unit 4**.

Fig. 1

Fig. 2

Fig. 3

Fig. 4

Flying Geese Unit
(make 24)

Unit 1
(make 2)

Unit 2
(make 4)

Unit 3
(make 2)

Unit 4

OCEAN WAVES

7 Sew **Unit 4** and 2 **Unit 2's** together to make **Unit 5**.

8 Sew **Unit 5** and 2 **Unit 2's** together to make **Unit 6**.

9 Sew **Unit 6** and 2 **Unit 3's** together as shown in **Block Assembly** to complete **Block**.

Unit 5

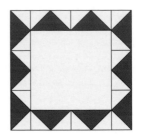

Unit 6

Block Assembly

Block

OCEAN WAVES

OHIO STAR

CUTTING OUT THE PIECES

From tan print fabric:
- Cut 2 **large squares** $5^{1}/_{4}"$ x $5^{1}/_{4}"$.
- Cut 4 **small squares** $4^{1}/_{2}"$ x $4^{1}/_{2}"$.

From green print fabric:
- Cut 2 **large squares** $5^{1}/_{4}"$ x $5^{1}/_{4}"$.

From rust checked fabric:
- Cut 1 **small square** $4^{1}/_{2}"$ x $4^{1}/_{2}"$.

Use ¹/₄" seam allowances throughout.

1 Draw diagonal lines from corner to corner in both directions on wrong side of each tan **large square**. With right sides together, place 1 tan **large square** on top of 1 green **large square**. Stitch seam ¹/₄" from each side of 1 drawn line (**Fig. 1**). Press stitching. Cut apart along drawn line (**Fig. 2**) to make 2 **Triangle-Squares**. Make 4 **Triangle-Squares**.

2 On wrong side of 2 **Triangle-Squares**, extend drawn line from corner of tan triangle to corner of green triangle.

3 Match 1 marked **Triangle-Square** and 1 unmarked **Triangle-Square** with contrasting fabrics facing and marked unit on top. Stitch seam ¹/₄" on each side of drawn line (**Fig. 3**). Cut apart along drawn line (**Fig. 4**) to make 2 **Hourglass Units**; press **Hourglass Units** open. Make 4 **Hourglass Units**.

Fig. 1

Fig. 2

Triangle-Squares
(make 4)

Fig. 3

Fig. 4

Hourglass Units
(make 4)

OHIO STAR

4 Sew 1 **Hourglass Unit** and 2 tan **small squares** together to make **Unit 1**. Make 2 **Unit 1's**.

5 Sew 2 **Hourglass Units** and rust **small square** together to make **Unit 2**.

6 Sew 2 **Unit 1's** and **Unit 2** together as shown in **Block Assembly** to complete **Block**.

Unit 1
(make 2)

Unit 2

Block Assembly

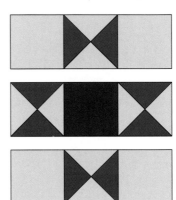

Block

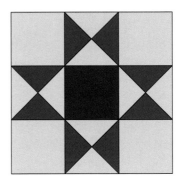

OHIO STAR

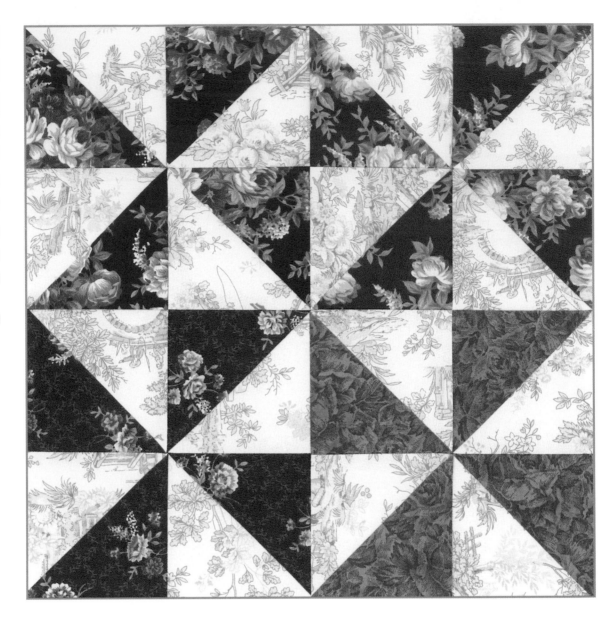

CUTTING OUT THE PIECES

From cream print fabric:
- Cut 8 **squares** $3^7/8$" x $3^7/8$".

From blue print fabric:
- Cut 2 **squares** $3^7/8$" x $3^7/8$".

From burgundy large print fabric:
- Cut 2 **squares** $3^7/8$" x $3^7/8$".

From burgundy small print fabric:
- Cut 2 **squares** $3^7/8$" x $3^7/8$".

From green print fabric:
- Cut 2 **squares** $3^7/8$" x $3^7/8$".

Use ¹/₄" seam allowances throughout.

1 Draw diagonal line (corner to corner) on wrong side of each cream **square**. With right sides together, place 1 cream **square** on top of 1 blue **square**. Stitch seam ¹/₄" from each side of drawn line (**Fig. 1**).

2 Cut along drawn line and press open to make 2 **Triangle-Squares**. Repeat with remaining **squares** to make 4 cream and blue **Triangle-Squares**, 4 cream and burgundy large print **Triangle-Squares**, 4 cream and green **Triangle-Squares**, and 4 cream and burgundy small print **Triangle-Squares.**

3 Sew 4 cream and blue **Triangle-Squares** together to make **Unit 1**.

4 Sew 4 cream and burgundy large print **Triangle-Squares** together to make **Unit 2**.

Fig. 1

Triangle-Squares
(make 4)

(make 4)

(make 4)

(make 4)

Unit 1

Unit 2

PINWHEEL

5 Sew 4 cream and green **Triangle-Squares** together to make **Unit 3**.

6 Sew 4 cream and small burgundy print **Triangle-Squares** together to make **Unit 4**.

7 Sew **Unit 1**, **Unit 2**, **Unit 3**, and **Unit 4** together as shown in **Block Assembly** to complete **Block**.

Unit 3

Unit 4

Block Assembly

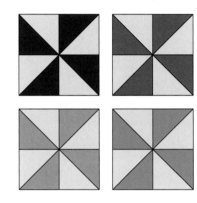

Block

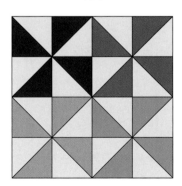

PINWHEEL

PINWHEEL AND SQUARES

CUTTING OUT THE PIECES

From cream print fabric:
- Cut 2 **medium squares** $2^7/8$" x $2^7/8$".
- Cut 20 **small squares** $2^1/2$" x $2^1/2$".

From blue print fabric:
- Cut 8 **small squares** $2^1/2$" x $2^1/2$".

From gold print fabric:
- Cut 2 **medium squares** $2^7/8$" x $2^7/8$".

From green print fabric:
- Cut 4 **large squares** $4^1/2$" x $4^1/2$".
- Cut 4 **rectangles** $4^1/2$" x $2^1/2$".

From burgundy print fabric:
- Cut 4 **small squares** $2^1/2$" x $2^1/2$".
- Cut 4 **rectangles** $4^1/2$" x $2^1/2$".

Use ¼" seam allowances throughout.

1 Draw diagonal line (corner to corner) on wrong side of each cream **medium square**. With right sides together, place 1 cream **medium square** on top of 1 gold **medium square**. Stitch seam ¼" from each side of drawn line (**Fig. 1**).

2 Cut along drawn line and press open to make 2 **Triangle-Squares**. Make 4 **Triangle-Squares**.

3 Sew 4 **Triangle-Squares** together to make **Unit 1**.

4 With right sides together, place 1 cream **small square** on 1 end of 1 green **rectangle** and stitch diagonally (**Fig. 2**). Trim ¼" from stitching line (**Fig. 3**). Open up and press, pressing seam allowance to darker fabric (**Fig. 4**).

5 Place another cream **small square** on opposite end of **rectangle**. Stitch and trim as shown in **Fig. 5**. Open up and press to complete **Flying Geese Unit A**. Make 4 **Flying Geese Unit A's**.

6 Repeat Steps 4 and 5 using burgundy **rectangles** and blue **small squares** to make 4 **Flying Geese Unit B's**.

Fig. 1

Triangle-Squares
(make 4)

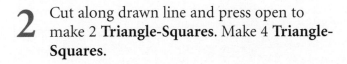

Unit 1

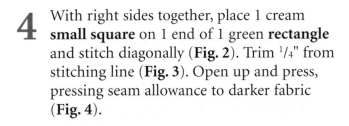

Fig. 2

Fig. 3

Fig. 4

Fig. 5

Flying Geese Unit A   **Flying Geese Unit B**
(make 4)   (make 4)

PINWHEEL AND SQUARES

7 Sew 1 **Flying Geese Unit A** and 1 **Flying Geese Unit B** together to make **Unit 2**. Make 4 **Unit 2's**.

8 With right sides together, place 1 cream **small square** on 1 corner of 1 **large square** and stitch diagonally (**Fig. 6**). Trim ¼" from stitching line (**Fig. 7**). Open up and press, pressing seam allowance to darker fabric (**Fig. 8**).

9 Add 2 more cream **small squares** and 1 burgundy **small square** to corners of **large square** as shown in **Fig. 9**. Open up and press to complete **Unit 3**. Make 4 **Unit 3's**.

10 Sew 2 **Unit 3's** and 1 **Unit 2** together to make **Unit 4**. Make 2 **Unit 4's**.

11 Sew 2 **Unit 2's** and **Unit 1** together to make **Unit 5**.

12 Sew 2 **Unit 4's** and **Unit 5** together as shown in **Block Assembly** to complete **Block**.

Unit 2
(make 4)

Fig. 6   Fig. 7

Fig. 8   Fig. 9

Unit 3
(make 4)

Unit 4   Unit 5
(make 2)

Block Assembly   Block

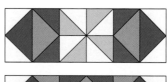 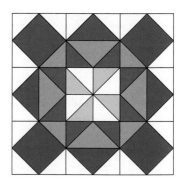

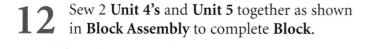

PINWHEEL AND SQUARES

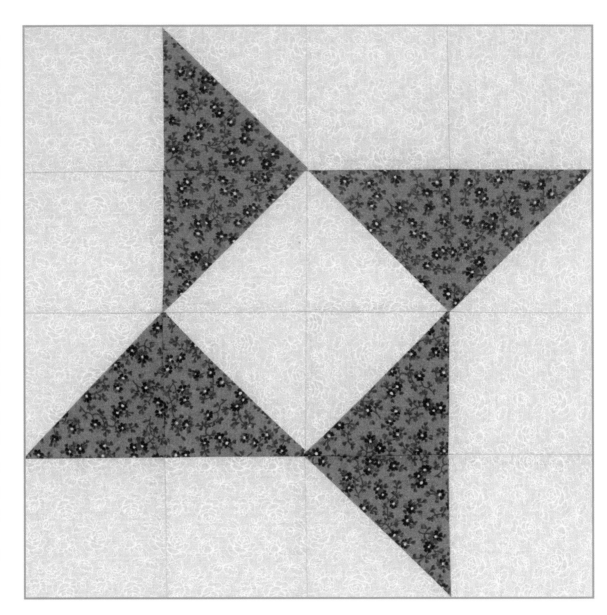

CUTTING OUT THE PIECES

From cream print fabric:
- Cut 4 **large squares** $3^7/_8$" x $3^7/_8$".
- Cut 8 **small squares** $3^1/_2$" x $3^1/_2$".

From teal print fabric:
- Cut 4 **large squares** $3^7/_8$" x $3^7/_8$".

156

Use ¹/₄" seam allowances throughout.

1 Draw diagonal line (corner to corner) on wrong side of each cream **large square**. With right sides together, place 1 cream **large square** on top of 1 teal **large square**. Stitch seam ¹/₄" from each side of drawn line (**Fig. 1**).

2 Cut along drawn line and press open to make 2 **Triangle-Squares**. Make 8 **Triangle-Squares**.

3 Sew 2 **Triangle-Squares** together to make **Unit 1**. Make 4 **Unit 1's**.

4 Sew 2 **small squares** together to make **Unit 2**. Make 4 **Unit 2's**.

Fig. 1

Triangle-Squares
(make 8)

Unit 1
(make 4)

Unit 2
(make 4)

PINWHEEL ASKEW

5 Sew 1 **Unit 1** and 1 **Unit 2** together to make **Unit 3**. Make 4 **Unit 3's**.

6 Sew 4 **Unit 3's** together as shown in **Block Assembly** to complete **Block**.

Unit 3
(make 4)

Block Assembly

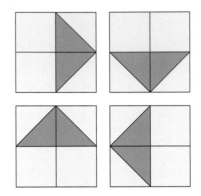

Block

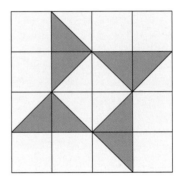

PINWHEEL ASKEW

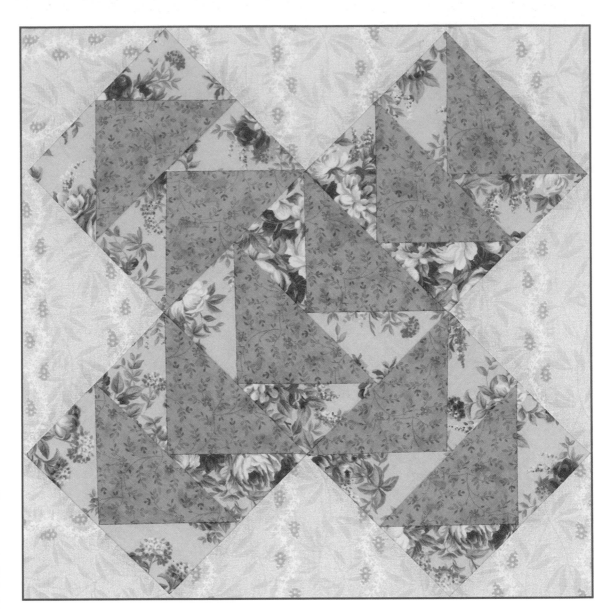

CUTTING OUT THE PIECES

From cream print fabric:
- Cut 1 square $7^1/_4$" x $7^1/_4$". Cut square *twice* diagonally for 4 **large triangles**.
- Cut 2 squares $3^7/_8$" x $3^7/_8$". Cut squares *once* diagonally for 4 **small triangles**.

From orange print fabric:
- Cut 10 **rectangles** $4^3/_4$" x $2^5/_8$".

From orange floral fabric:
- Cut 20 **squares** $2^5/_8$" x $2^5/_8$".

160

ASSEMBLING THE BLOCK

Use ¹/₄" seam allowances throughout.

1 With right sides together, place 1 **square** on 1 end of 1 **rectangle** and stitch diagonally (**Fig. 1**). Trim ¹/₄" from stitching line (**Fig. 2**). Open up and press, pressing seam allowance to darker fabric (**Fig. 3**).

2 Place another **square** on opposite end of **rectangle**. Stitch and trim as shown in **Fig. 4**. Open up and press to complete **Flying Geese Unit**. Make 10 **Flying Geese Units**.

3 Sew 6 **Flying Geese Units** together to make **Unit 1**.

4 Sew **Unit 1** and 2 **small triangles** together to make **Unit 2**.

Fig. 1

Fig. 2

Fig. 3

Fig. 4

Flying Geese Unit
(make 10)

Unit 1

Unit 2

RAILROAD CROSSING

5 Sew 2 **Flying Geese Units** and 1 **small triangle** together to make **Unit 3**. Make 2 **Unit 3's**.

6 Sew 1 **Unit 3** and 2 **large triangles** together to make **Unit 4**. Make 2 **Unit 4's**.

7 Sew **Unit 2** and 2 **Unit 4's** together as shown in **Block Assembly** to complete **Block**.

Unit 3
(make 2)

Unit 4
(make 2)

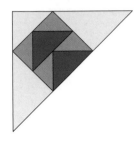

Block Assembly

Block

RAILROAD CROSSING

CUTTING OUT THE PIECES

From tan print fabric:
- Cut 6 **medium squares** $2^7/8$" x $2^7/8$".
- Cut 4 **small squares** $2^1/2$" x $2^1/2$".
- Cut 8 **rectangles** $4^1/2$" x $2^1/2$".

From green print fabric:
- Cut 1 **large square** $4^1/2$" x $4^1/2$".
- Cut 6 **medium squares** $2^7/8$" x $2^7/8$".
- Cut 8 **small squares** $2^1/2$" x $2^1/2$".

Use ¹/₄" seam allowances throughout.

1 Draw diagonal line (corner to corner) on wrong side of each tan **medium square**. With right sides together, place 1 tan **medium square** on top of 1 green **medium square**. Stitch seam ¹/₄" from each side of drawn line (**Fig. 1**).

2 Cut along drawn line and press open to make 2 **Triangle-Squares**. Make 12 **Triangle-Squares**.

3 Sew 3 **Triangle-Squares** and 1 tan **small square** together to make **Unit 1**. Make 4 **Unit 1's**.

4 With right sides together, place 1 green **small square** on 1 end of 1 **rectangle** and stitch diagonally (**Fig. 2**). Trim ¹/₄" from stitching line (**Fig. 3**). Open up and press, pressing seam allowance to darker fabric (**Fig. 4**).

5 Place another green **small square** on opposite end of **rectangle**. Stitch and trim as shown in **Fig. 5**. Open up and press to complete **Flying Geese Unit**. Make 4 **Flying Geese Units**.

Fig. 1

Triangle-Squares
(make 12)

Unit 1
(make 4)

Fig. 2

Fig. 3

Fig. 4

Fig. 5

Flying Geese Unit
(make 4)

ROBBING PETER TO PAY PAUL

6 Sew 1 **Flying Geese Unit** and 1 **rectangle** together to make **Unit 2**. Make 4 **Unit 2's**.

7 Sew 2 **Unit 1's** and 1 **Unit 2** together to make **Unit 3**. Make 2 **Unit 3's**.

8 Sew 2 **Unit 2's** and **large square** together to make **Unit 4**.

9 Sew 2 **Unit 3's** and **Unit 4** together as shown in **Block Assembly** to complete **Block**.

Unit 2
(make 4)

Unit 3
(make 2)

Unit 4

Block Assembly

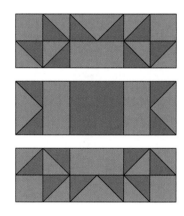

Block

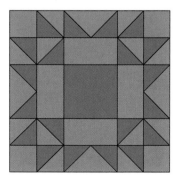

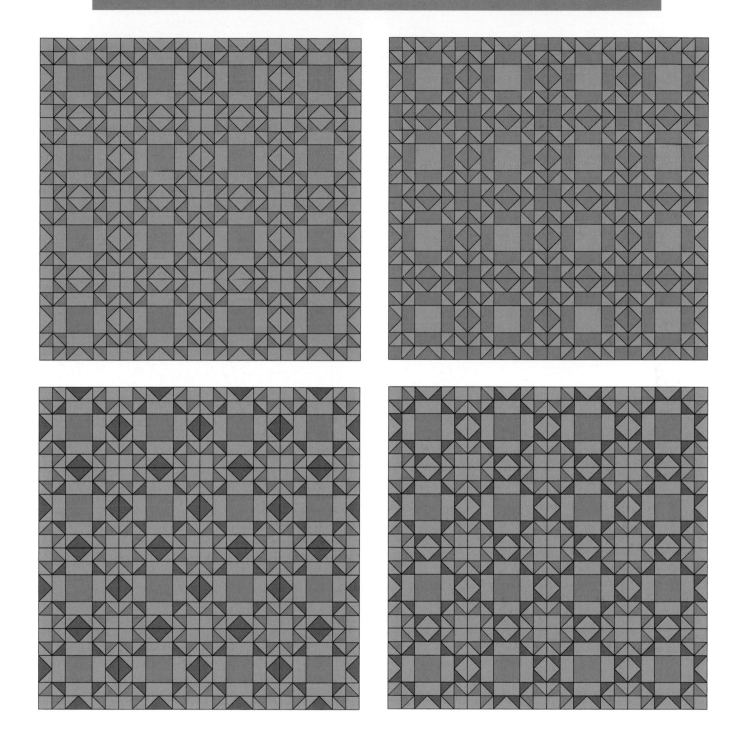

CUTTING OUT THE PIECES

From cream print fabric:
- Cut 1 **large square** $4^1/2$" x $4^1/2$".
- Cut 12 **small squares** $2^1/2$" x $2^1/2$".

From blue print fabric:
- Cut 4 **large squares** $4^1/2$" x $4^1/2$".
- Cut 4 **rectangles** $4^1/2$" x $2^1/2$".

From green print fabric:
- Cut 4 **small squares** $2^1/2$" x $2^1/2$".

From pink print fabric:
- Cut 4 **rectangles** $4^1/2$" x $2^1/2$".

Use ¹/₄" seam allowances throughout.

1 With right sides together, place 1 cream **small square** on 1 corner of 1 blue **large square** and stitch diagonally (**Fig. 1**). Trim ¹/₄" from stitching line (**Fig. 2**). Open up and press, pressing seam allowance to darker fabric (**Fig. 3**).

2 Add 2 more cream **small squares** and 1 green **small square** to corners of blue **large square** as shown in **Fig. 4**. Open up and press to complete **Unit 1**. Make 4 **Unit 1's**.

3 Sew 1 blue **rectangle** and 1 pink **rectangle** together to make **Unit 2**. Make 4 **Unit 2's**.

Fig. 1

Fig. 2

Fig. 3

Fig. 4

Unit 1
(make 4)

Unit 2
(make 4)

4 Sew 2 **Unit 1's** and 1 **Unit 2** together to make **Unit 3**. Make 2 **Unit 3's**.

5 Sew 2 **Unit 2's** and cream **large square** together to make **Unit 4**.

6 Sew 2 **Unit 3's** and **Unit 4** together as shown in **Block Assembly** to complete **Block**.

Unit 3
(make 2)

Unit 4

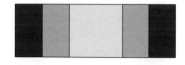

Block Assembly

Block

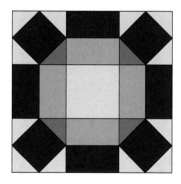

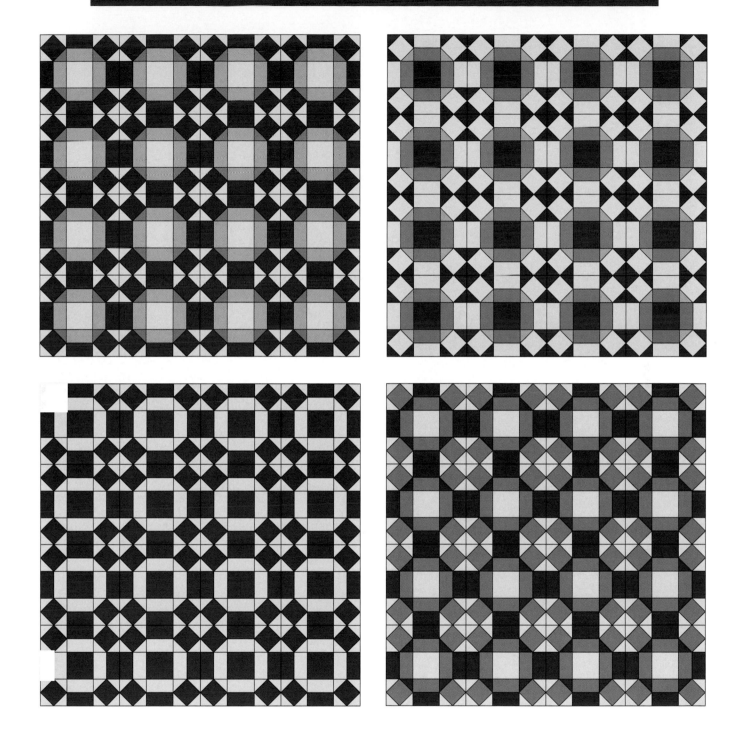

ROLLING STONE

CUTTING OUT THE PIECES

From tan print fabric:
- Cut 4 **squares** $2^7/_8$" x $2^7/_8$".
- Cut 2 squares $2^7/_8$" x $2^7/_8$". Cut squares *once* diagonally to make 4 **small triangles**.

From burgundy print fabric:
- Cut 4 **squares** $2^7/_8$" x $2^7/_8$".

From green print fabric:
- Cut 2 squares $4^7/_8$" x $4^7/_8$". Cut squares *once* diagonally to make 4 **medium triangles**.

From pink print fabric:
- Cut 2 squares $6^7/_8$" x $6^7/_8$". Cut squares *once* diagonally to make 4 **large triangles**.

Use ¹/₄" seam allowances throughout.

1 Draw diagonal line (corner to corner) on wrong side of each tan **square**. With right sides together, place 1 tan **square** on top of 1 burgundy **square**. Stitch seam ¹/₄" from each side of drawn line (**Fig. 1**).

2 Cut along drawn line and press open to make 2 **Triangle-Squares**. Make 8 **Triangle-Squares**.

3 Sew 2 **Triangle-Squares** and 1 **small triangle** together to make **Unit 1**. Make 4 **Unit 1's**.

4 Sew 1 **Unit 1** and 1 **medium triangle** together to make **Unit 2**. Make 4 **Unit 2's**.

Fig. 1

Triangle-squares
(make 8)

Unit 1
(make 4)

Unit 2
(make 4)

ROSEBUD

5 Sew 1 **Unit 2** and 1 **large triangle** together to make **Unit 3**. Make 4 **Unit 3's**.

6 Sew 4 **Unit 3's** together as shown in **Block Assembly** to complete **Block**.

Unit 3
(make 4)

Block Assembly

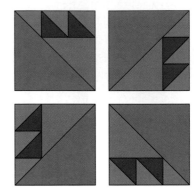

Block

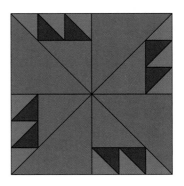

174

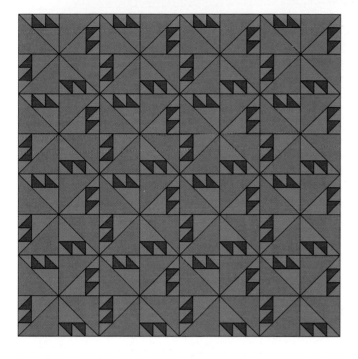

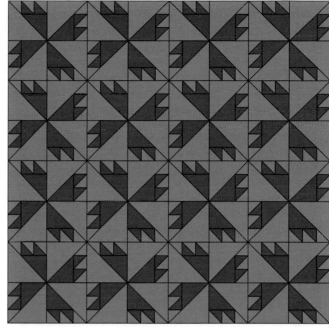

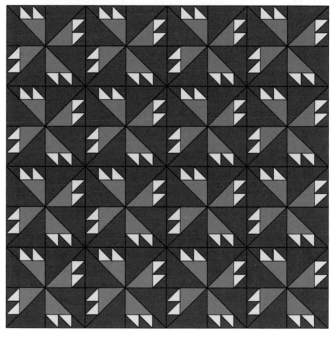

ROSEBUD

SAWTOOTH PATCHWORK

CUTTING OUT THE PIECES

From cream print fabric:
- Cut 16 **small squares** $2^1/2$" x $2^1/2$".

From green print fabric:
- Cut 5 **medium squares** $4^1/2$" x $4^1/2$".

From gold print fabric:
- Cut 2 **large squares** $4^7/8$" x $4^7/8$".
- Cut 4 **small squares** $2^1/2$" x $2^1/2$".

From blue print fabric:
- Cut 2 **large squares** $4^7/8$" x $4^7/8$".

176

Use ¹/₄" seam allowances throughout.

1 Draw diagonal line (corner to corner) on wrong side of each gold **large square**. With right sides together, place 1 gold **large square** on top of 1 blue **large square**. Stitch seam ¹/₄" from each side of drawn line (**Fig. 1**).

2 Cut along drawn line and press open to make 2 **Triangle-Squares**. Make 4 **Triangle-Squares**.

3 With right sides together, place 1 cream **small square** on 1 corner of 1 **medium square** and stitch diagonally (**Fig. 2**). Trim ¹/₄" from stitching line (**Fig. 3**). Open up and press, pressing seam allowance to darker fabric (**Fig. 4**).

4 Continue adding cream **small squares** to corners of **medium square** as shown in **Fig. 5**. Open up and press to complete **Unit 1**. Make 4 **Unit 1's**.

Fig. 1

Triangle-Squares
(make 4)

Fig. 2

Fig. 3

Fig. 4

Fig. 5

Unit 1
(make 4)

177

SAWTOOTH PATCHWORK

5 Repeat Steps 3 and 4 using 4 gold **small squares** and 1 **medium square** to make **Unit 2**.

6 Sew 2 **Triangle-Squares** and 1 **Unit 1** together to make **Unit 3**. Make 2 **Unit 3's**.

7 Sew 2 **Unit 1's** and **Unit 2** together to make **Unit 4**.

8 Sew 2 **Unit 3's** and **Unit 4** together as shown in **Block Assembly** to complete **Block**.

Unit 2

Unit 3
(make 2)

Unit 4

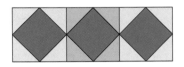

Block Assembly

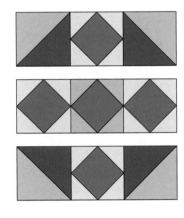

Block

SAWTOOTH PATCHWORK

SHOO-FLY

CUTTING OUT THE PIECES

From tan print fabric:
- Cut 2 **large squares** $4^7/_8$" x $4^7/_8$".
- Cut 4 **small squares** $4^1/_2$" x $4^1/_2$".

From dark green print fabric:
- Cut 2 **large squares** $4^7/_8$" x $4^7/_8$".

From light green print fabric:
- Cut 1 **small square** $4^1/_2$" x $4^1/_2$".

Use ¹/₄" seam allowances throughout.

1 Draw diagonal line (corner to corner) on wrong side of each tan **large square**. With right sides together, place 1 tan **large square** on top of 1 dark green **large square**. Stitch seam ¹/₄" from each side of drawn line (**Fig. 1**).

2 Cut along drawn line and press open to make 2 **Triangle-Squares**. Make 4 **Triangle-Squares**.

3 Sew 2 **Triangle-Squares** and 1 tan **small square** together to make **Unit 1**. Make 2 **Unit 1's.**

Fig. 1

Triangle-Squares
(make 4)

Unit 1
(make 2)

SHOO-FLY

4 Sew 2 tan **small squares** and light green **small square** together to make **Unit 2.**

5 Sew 2 **Unit 1's** and **Unit 2** together as shown in **Block Assembly** to complete **Block.**

Unit 2

Block Assembly

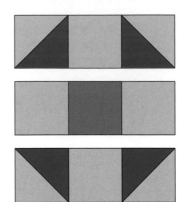

Block

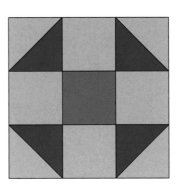

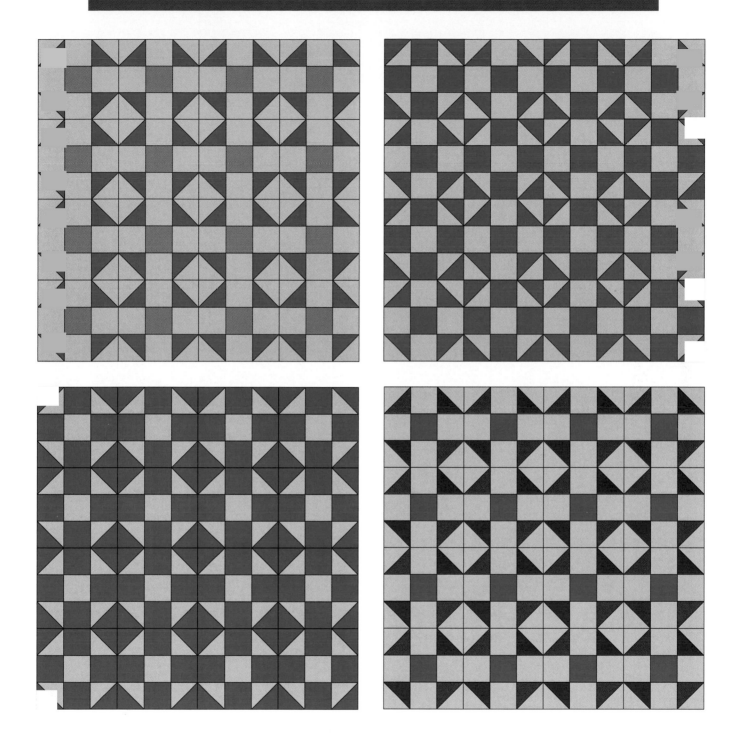

183

SQUARE AND STAR

CUTTING OUT THE PIECES

From cream print fabric:
- Cut 4 **medium squares** $4^{1}/_{4}$" x $4^{1}/_{4}$".
- Cut 4 **small squares** $3^{1}/_{2}$" x $3^{1}/_{2}$".

From gold print fabric:
- Cut 1 **large square** $6^{1}/_{2}$" x $6^{1}/_{2}$".
- Cut 2 **medium squares** $4^{1}/_{4}$" x $4^{1}/_{4}$".

From green print fabric:
- Cut 2 **medium squares** $4^{1}/_{4}$" x $4^{1}/_{4}$".
- Cut 4 **small squares** $3^{1}/_{2}$" x $3^{1}/_{2}$".

Use ¹/₄" seam allowances throughout.

1 With right sides together, place 1 green **small square** on 1 corner of **large square** and stitch diagonally (**Fig. 1**). Trim ¹/₄" from stitching line (**Fig. 2**). Open up and press, pressing seam allowance to darker fabric (**Fig. 3**).

2 Continue adding green **small squares** to corners of **large square** as shown in **Fig. 4**. Open up and press to complete **Unit 1**.

3 Draw diagonal line (corner to corner) on wrong side of each cream **medium square**. With right sides together, place 1 cream **medium square** on top of 1 green **medium square**. Stitch seam ¹/₄" from each side of drawn line (**Fig. 5**).

4 Cut along drawn line and press open to make 2 **Triangle-Squares**. Repeat with remaining **medium squares** to make 4 cream and green **Triangle-Squares** and 4 cream and gold **Triangle-Squares**.

5 On wrong side of cream and gold **Triangle-Squares**, extend drawn line from corner of cream triangle to corner of gold triangle.

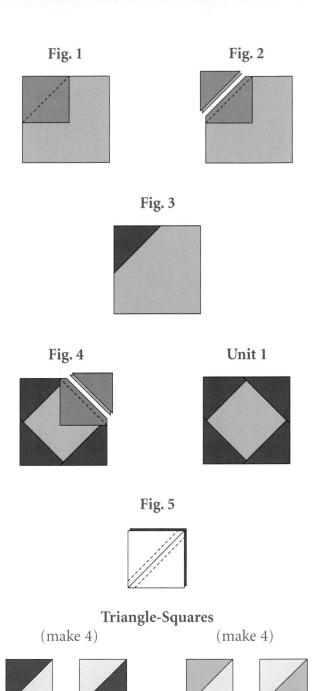

Fig. 1

Fig. 2

Fig. 3

Fig. 4

Unit 1

Fig. 5

Triangle-Squares
(make 4)   (make 4)

185

SQUARE AND STAR

6 Match 1 cream and gold **Triangle-Square** and 1 cream and green **Triangle-Square** with green and gold triangles facing cream triangles and marked unit on top. Stitch seam $^1/_4$" on each side of drawn line (**Fig. 6**). Cut apart along drawn line (**Fig. 7**) to make 2 **Hourglass Units**; press **Hourglass Units** open. Make 8 **Hourglass Units**.

7 Sew 2 **Hourglass Units** together to make **Unit 2**. Make 4 **Unit 2's**.

8 Sew 1 **Unit 2** and 2 cream **small squares** together to make **Unit 3**. Make 2 **Unit 3's**.

9 Sew **Unit 1** and 2 **Unit 2's** together to make **Unit 4**.

10 Sew 2 **Unit 3's** and **Unit 4** together as shown in **Block Assembly** to complete **Block**.

Fig. 6

Fig. 7

Hourglass Units
(make 8)

Unit 2
(make 4)

Unit 3
(make 2)

Unit 4

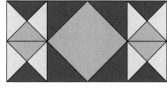

Block Assembly

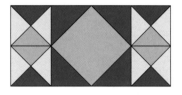

Block

187

SQUARE AND STAR

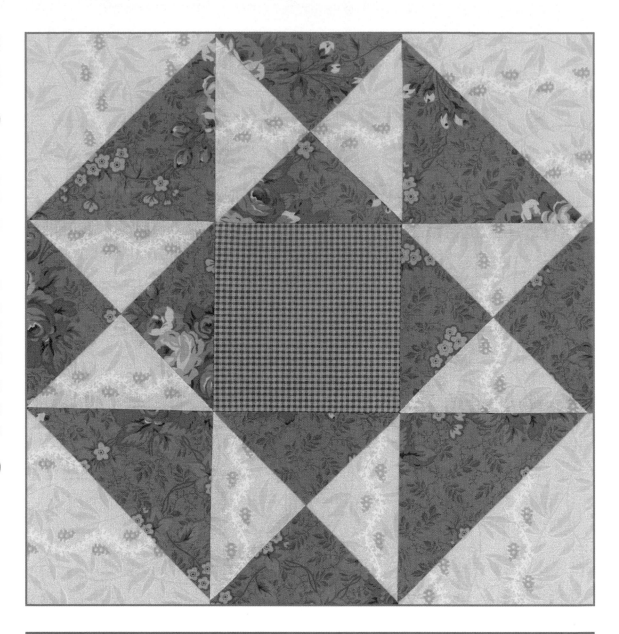

SWAMP ANGEL

CUTTING OUT THE PIECES

From tan print fabric:
- Cut 2 **large squares** $5^1/4$" x $5^1/4$".
- Cut 2 **medium squares** $4^7/8$" x $4^7/8$".

From pink print fabric:
- Cut 2 **large squares** $5^1/4$" x $5^1/4$".
- Cut 2 **medium squares** $4^7/8$" x $4^7/8$".

From green checked fabric:
- Cut 1 **small square** $4^1/2$" x $4^1/2$".

Use ¹/₄" seam allowances throughout.

1 Draw diagonal line (corner to corner) on wrong side of each tan **medium square**. With right sides together, place 1 tan **medium square** on top of 1 pink **medium square**. Stitch seam ¹/₄" from each side of drawn line (**Fig. 1**).

2 Cut along drawn line and press open to make 2 **Small Triangle-Squares**. Make 4 **Small Triangle-Squares**.

3 Draw diagonal lines from corner to corner in both directions on wrong side of each tan **large square**. With right sides together, place 1 tan **large square** on top of 1 pink **large square**. Stitch seam ¹/₄" from each side of 1 drawn line (**Fig. 2**). Press stitching. Cut apart along drawn line (**Fig. 3**) to make 2 **Large Triangle-Squares**; press open. Make 4 **Large Triangle-Squares**.

4 On wrong side of 2 **Large Triangle-Squares**, extend drawn line from corner of tan triangle to corner of pink triangle.

5 Match 1 marked **Triangle-Square** and 1 unmarked **Large Triangle-Square** with contrasting fabrics facing and marked unit on top. Stitch seam ¹/₄" on each side of drawn line (**Fig. 4**). Cut apart along drawn line (**Fig. 5**) to make 2 **Hourglass Units**; press hourglass units open. Make 4 **Hourglass Units**.

Fig. 1

Small Triangle-Squares
(make 4)

Fig. 2   Fig. 3

Large Triangle-Squares
(make 4)

Fig. 4   Fig. 5

Hourglass Units
(make 4)

SWAMP ANGEL

6 Sew 2 **Small Triangle-Squares** and 1 **Hourglass Unit** together to make **Unit 1**. Make 2 **Unit 1's**.

7 Sew 2 **Hourglass Units** and **small square** together to make **Unit 2**.

8 Sew 2 **Unit 1's** and **Unit 2** together as shown in **Block Assembly** to complete **Block**.

Unit 1
(make 2)

Unit 2

Block Assembly

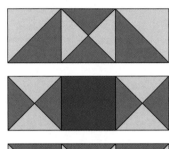

Block

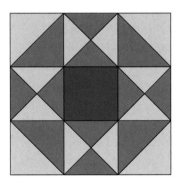

SWAMP ANGEL

CUTTING OUT THE PIECES

From cream print fabric:
- Cut 4 **large squares** $3^3/8$" x $3^3/8$".
- Cut 4 **medium squares** $2^7/8$" x $2^7/8$".
- Cut 4 **rectangles** $4^1/2$" x $2^1/2$".

From blue print fabric:
- Cut 4 **small squares** $2^1/2$" x $2^1/2$".
- Cut 1 square $5^1/4$" x $5^1/4$". Cut square *twice* diagonally to make 4 **large triangles**.

From pink print fabric:
- Cut 1 **large square** $3^3/8$" x $3^3/8$".
- Cut 4 **medium squares** $2^7/8$" x $2^7/8$".
- Cut 8 **small squares** $2^1/2$" x $2^1/2$".
- Cut 2 squares $2^7/8$" x $2^7/8$". Cut squares *once* diagonally to make 4 **small triangles**.

Use ¹/₄" seam allowances throughout.

1 Sew 2 **small triangles**, 2 cream **large squares**, and pink **large square** together to make **Unit 1**.

2 Sew 2 **large triangles** and 1 cream **large square** together to make **Unit 2**. Make 2 **Unit 2's**.

3 Sew **Unit 1**, 2 **Unit 2's**, and 2 **small triangles** together to make **Unit 3**.

4 Draw diagonal line (corner to corner) on wrong side of each cream **medium square**. With right sides together, place 1 cream **medium square** on top of 1 pink **medium square**. Stitch seam ¹/₄" from each side of drawn line (**Fig. 1**).

5 Cut along drawn line and press open to make 2 **Triangle-Squares**. Make 8 **Triangle-Squares**.

6 With right sides together, place 1 pink **small square** on 1 end of 1 **rectangle** and stitch diagonally (**Fig. 2**). Trim ¹/₄" from stitching line (**Fig. 3**). Open up and press, pressing seam allowance to darker fabric (**Fig. 4**).

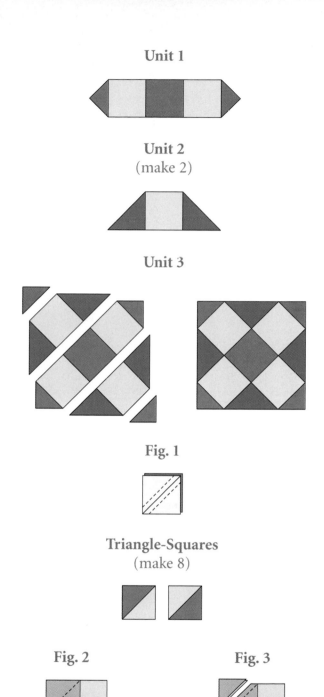

Unit 1

Unit 2
(make 2)

Unit 3

Fig. 1

Triangle-Squares
(make 8)

Fig. 2

Fig. 3

Fig. 4

7 Place another pink **small square** on opposite end of **rectangle**. Stitch and trim as shown in **Fig. 5**. Open up and press to complete **Flying Geese Unit**. Make 4 **Flying Geese Units**.

8 Sew 2 **Triangle-Squares** and 1 **Flying Geese Unit** together to make **Unit 4**. Make 4 **Unit 4's**.

9 Sew 1 blue **small square** to each end of 2 **Unit 4's** to make 2 **Unit 5's**.

10 Sew **Unit 3**, 2 **Unit 4's**, then 2 **Unit 5's** together as shown in **Block Assembly** to complete **Block**.

Fig. 5

Flying Geese Unit
(make 4)

Unit 4
(make 4)

Unit 5
(make 2)

Block Assembly

Block

SWING IN THE CENTER

VARIABLE STAR

CUTTING OUT THE PIECES

From cream print fabric:
- Cut 1 **large square** $6^1/2$" x $6^1/2$".
- Cut 4 **small squares** $3^1/2$" x $3^1/2$".
- Cut 4 **rectangles** $6^1/2$" x $3^1/2$".

From gold print fabric:
- Cut 4 **small squares** $3^1/2$" x $3^1/2$".

From green checked fabric:
- Cut 8 **small squares** $3^1/2$" x $3^1/2$".

Use ¹/₄" seam allowances throughout.

1 With right sides together, place 1 green **small square** on 1 end of 1 **rectangle** and stitch diagonally (**Fig. 1**). Trim ¹/₄" from stitching line (**Fig. 2**). Open up and press, pressing seam allowance to darker fabric (**Fig. 3**).

2 Place another green **small square** on opposite end of **rectangle**. Stitch and trim as shown in **Fig. 4**. Open up and press to complete **Flying Geese Unit**. Make 4 **Flying Geese Units**.

3 Sew 1 **Flying Geese Unit** and 2 cream **small squares** together to make **Unit 1**. Make 2 **Unit 1's**.

4 With right sides together, place 1 gold **small square** on 1 corner of **large square** and stitch diagonally (**Fig. 5**). Trim ¹/₄" from stitching line (**Fig. 6**). Open up and press, pressing seam allowance to darker fabric (**Fig. 7**).

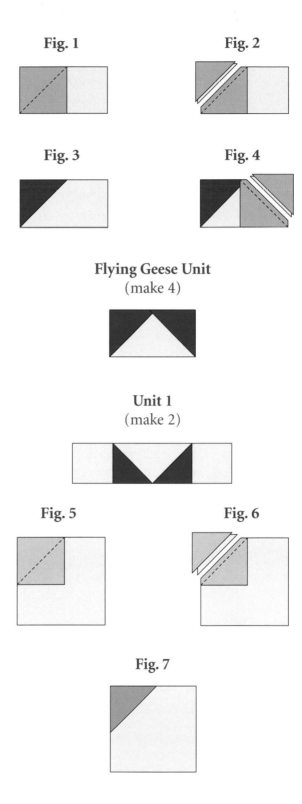

Fig. 1

Fig. 2

Fig. 3

Fig. 4

Flying Geese Unit
(make 4)

Unit 1
(make 2)

Fig. 5

Fig. 6

Fig. 7

VARIABLE STAR

5 Continue adding gold **small squares** to corners of **large square** as shown in **Fig. 8**. Open up and press to complete **Unit 2**.

6 Sew 2 **Flying Geese Units** and **Unit 2** together to complete **Unit 3**.

7 Sew 2 **Unit 1's** and **Unit 3** together as shown in **Block Assembly** to complete **Block**.

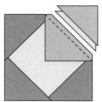

Fig. 8

Unit 2

Unit 3

Block Assembly

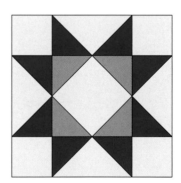

Block

VARIABLE STAR

WEATHER VANE

CUTTING OUT THE PIECES

From cream print fabric:
- Cut 4 **medium squares** 2⁷/₈" x 2⁷/₈".
- Cut 8 **small squares** 2¹/₂" x 2¹/₂".

From green print fabric:
- Cut 1 **large square** 4¹/₂" x 4¹/₂".

From teal print fabric:
- Cut 8 **rectangles** 4¹/₂" x 2¹/₂".

From gold print fabric:
- Cut 4 **medium squares** 2⁷/₈" x 2⁷/₈".
- Cut 4 **small squares** 2¹/₂" x 2¹/₂".

From burgundy floral fabric:
- Cut 4 **small squares** 2¹/₂" x 2¹/₂".

Use ¹/₄" seam allowances throughout.

1 Draw diagonal line (corner to corner) on wrong side of each cream **medium square**. With right sides together, place 1 cream **medium square** on top of 1 gold **medium square**. Stitch seam ¹/₄" from each side of drawn line (**Fig. 1**).

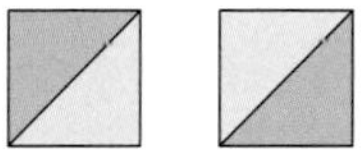

2 Cut along drawn line and press open to make 2 **Triangle-Squares**. Make 8 **Triangle-Squares**.

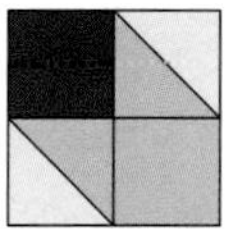

3 Sew 2 **Triangle-Squares**, 1 burgundy **small square**, and 1 gold **small square** together to make **Unit 1**. Make 4 **Unit 1's**.

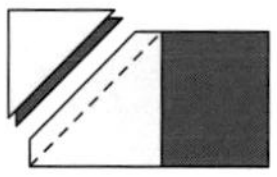

4 With right sides together, place 1 cream **small square** on 1 end of 1 **rectangle** and stitch diagonally (**Fig. 2**). Trim ¹/₄" from stitching line (**Fig. 3**). Open up and press, pressing seam allowance to darker fabric (**Fig. 4**).

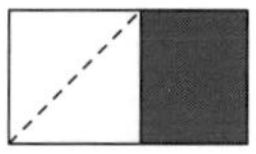

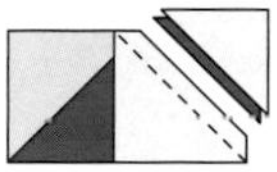

5 Place another cream **small square** on opposite end of **rectangle**. Stitch and trim as shown in **Fig. 5**. Open up and press to complete **Flying Geese Unit**. Make 4 **Flying Geese Units**.

Fig. 1

Triangle-Squares
(make 8)

Unit 1
(make 4)

Fig. 2

Fig. 3

Fig. 4

Fig. 5

Flying Geese Unit
(make 4)

WEATHER VANE

6 Sew 1 **Flying Geese Unit** and 1 **rectangle** together to make **Unit 2**. Make 4 **Unit 2's**.

Unit 2
(make 4)

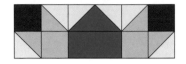

7 Sew 2 **Unit 1's** and 1 **Unit 2** together to make **Unit 3**. Make 2 **Unit 3's**.

Unit 3
(make 2)

8 Sew 2 **Unit 2's** and **large square** together to make **Unit 4**.

Unit 4

9 Sew 2 **Unit 3's** and **Unit 4** together as shown in **Block Assembly** to complete **Block**.

Block Assembly

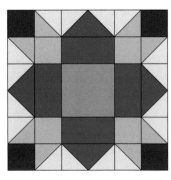

Block

202

WEATHER VANE

Break out those fat quarters you've been collecting or head for the fabric shop! Make this Sensational Sampler Quilt as shown, or design your own!

Finished Size: 74^1/$_2$" x 88^3/$_4$" (189 cm x 225 cm)

*You may use the **blocks** shown (also listed on page 206), or choose any combination of 30 **blocks** to make your **Sensational Sampler Quilt**. Once you've completed your **blocks**, lay them out on the floor. You may wish to rearrange the **blocks**, balancing the colors and block designs to achieve the desired look. **Sampler Quilt** variations are shown on page 208. If you'd like to make a different size quilt, refer to the chart on page 209. Refer to **Borders**, page 240, if you wish to add squared or mitered borders.*

YARDAGE REQUIREMENTS

*Yardage requirements do not include **blocks**.*

    3^1/$_8$ yds (2.9 m) of cream print fabric
    ^{1}/$_4$ yd (23 cm) of green print fabric
    1 yd (91 cm) of fabric for binding
    5^1/$_2$ yds (5 m) of fabric for backing
    82" x 96" (208 cm x 244 cm) piece of batting

CUTTING OUT THE SASHINGS AND BINDING

Vertical and horizontal sashings are listed separately in case you use a directional print.

From cream print fabric:

- Cut 12 **strips** 2^3/$_4$"w. From these strips, cut 35 **horizontal sashings** 12^1/$_2$" x 2^3/$_4$".
- Cut 3 strips 12^1/$_2$"w. From these strips, cut 36 **vertical sashings** 2^3/$_4$" x 12^1/$_2$".
- Cut **square for binding** 31" x 31".

From green print fabric:

- Cut 3 strips 2^3/$_4$"w. From these strips, cut 42 **sashing squares** 2^3/$_4$" x 2^3/$_4$".

ASSEMBLING THE QUILT

Use ¹/₄" seam allowances throughout.

1 Sew 5 **Blocks** and 6 **vertical sashings** together to make **Row**. Make 6 **Rows**.

2 Sew 5 **horizontal sashings** and 6 **sashing squares** together to make **Sashing Row**. Make 7 **Sashing Rows**.

3 Alternate and sew **Sashing Rows** and **Rows** together to complete quilt top.

COMPLETING THE QUILT

1 Following **Quilting**, page 243, to mark, layer, and quilt as desired. Our quilt is machine quilted. The **sashings** are quilted with the same design, but each **block** is quilted differently.

2 Using **square for binding**, follow **Binding**, page 248, to bind quilt using 2¹/₂"w bias binding with mitered corners.

Row (make 6)

Sashing Row (make 7)

Quilt Top Diagram

BLOCKS USED IN OUR SAMPLER QUILT

Row 1: *Fox and Geese, page 84; Navajo, page 132; Basket, page 8; Flying Dutchman, page 80; Dove-in-the-Window, page 64*

Row 2: *Swing in the Center, page 192; Mrs. Bryan's Choice, page 128; Cut Glass Dish, page 56; Gentleman's Fancy, page 88; Robbing Peter to Pay Paul, page 164*

Row 3: *Variable Star, page 196; Corn and Beans, page 44; Laurel Wreath, page 108; Hen and Chicks, page 96; Swamp Angel, page 188*

Row 4: *Magic Triangles, page 116; Rolling Stone, page 168; Railroad Crossing, page 160; Jacob's Ladder, page 100; Cat's Cradle, page 28*

Row 5: *Pinwheel, page 148; Rosebud, page 172; Crow's Foot, page 52; Ocean Waves, page 140; Golgotha, page 92*

Row 6: *Card Trick, page 24; Flutter Wheel, page 76; Boxes, page 12; Ohio Star, page 144; Churn Dash, page 40*

SENSATIONAL SAMPLER

Quilt Top Diagram Variation #1

*There are 15 different **blocks** in this diagram. Each block is used twice, but in different color schemes. Can you find the 15 pairs of **blocks**?*

Quilt Top Diagram Variation #2

*The **blocks** used in our **Sensational Sampler** are shown here in reds and creams. Other classic two-color combinations, such as blues and yellows or navies and whites, make stunning quilts.*

SENSATIONAL SAMPLER
OPTIONAL QUILT SIZES

Number of Blocks	Horizontal Sashings	Vertical Sashings	Sashing Squares	Size of Blocks and Sashings
3 x 3	12	12	16	45" x 45"
3 x 4	15	16	20	45" x 59^1/$_4$"
3 x 5	18	20	24	45" x 73^1/$_2$"
4 x 4	20	20	25	59^1/$_4$" x 59^1/$_4$"
4 x 5	24	25	30	59^1/$_4$" x 73^1/$_2$"
4 x 6	28	30	35	59^1/$_4$" x 87^3/$_4$"
5 x 5	30	30	36	73^1/$_2$" x 73^1/$_2$"
5 x 6	35	36	42	73^1/$_2$" x 87^3/$_4$"
5 x 7	40	42	48	73^1/$_2$" x 102"
6 x 7	48	49	56	87^3/$_4$" x 102"
7 x 7	56	56	64	102" x 102"

Sizes of mattress tops:

Crib: 27" x 52"

Twin: 39" x 75"

Full: 54" x 75"

Queen: 60" x 80"

King 76" x 80"

*T*o determine **width** of quilt for your bed, add the width of mattress top and twice the depth of mattress–or depth you wish quilt to hang from bed top. To determine **length** of quilt, add the length of mattress top and depth of mattress or depth you wish quilt to hang at foot-of-bed. Add extra to length for pillow tuck, if desired.

DYNAMIC DUO WALL HANGING

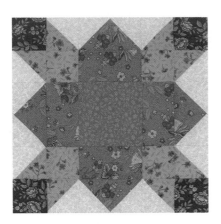

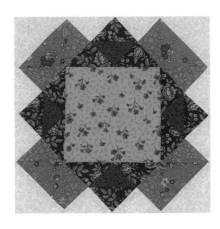

Made from a coordinated fabric line, this Dynamic Duo Wall Hanging is sure to brighten any room. Mix and match your blocks AND mix and match your fabrics!

Finished Size: 45" x 45" (114 cm x 114 cm)

*Our wall hanging uses 5 **Weather Vane Blocks** (page 200) and 4 **Flower Pot Blocks** (page 72). See our suggestions for other great combinations on pages 214 - 216, or choose your favorites. The chart on page 213 provides information for making different size quilts using your **Dynamic Duo!***

YARDAGE REQUIREMENTS

Yardages are based on our choice of blocks. Cut borders and binding before cutting block pieces.

- $3/4$ yd (69 cm) of cream print fabric
- $1^1/2$ yds (1.4 m) of green print fabric
- $5/8$ yd (57 cm) of gold print fabric
- $3/8$ yd (34 cm) of burgundy floral fabric
- $1/8$ yd (11 cm) of burgundy print fabric
- $5/8$ yd (57 cm) of teal print fabric
- $1^1/2$ yds (1.4 m) of cream and teal print fabric
- 3 yds (2.7 m) for backing
- 53" x 53" (135 cm x 135 cm) square of batting

CUTTING OUT THE BORDERS AND BINDING
From green print fabric:
- Cut 4 *lengthwise* **inner borders** $1^1/4$" x 48".
- Cut **square for binding** 24" x 24".

From cream and teal print fabric:
- Cut 4 *lengthwise* **outer borders** $3^3/4$" x 48".

ASSEMBLING THE WALL HANGING

Use ¹/₄" seam allowances throughout.

1 Sew 2 **Weather Vane Blocks** and 1 **Flower Pot Block** together to make **Row A**. Make 2 **Row A's**.

2 Sew 1 **Weather Vane Block** and 2 **Flower Pot Blocks** together to make **Row B**.

3 Sew **Rows** together to complete center section of wall hanging.

4 Sew 1 **inner border** and 1 **outer border** together lengthwise. Repeat with remaining **borders**. Follow **Adding Mitered Borders**, page 240, to add borders to wall hanging.

COMPLETING THE WALL HANGING

1 Following **Quilting**, page 243, to mark, layer, and quilt as desired. Our wall hanging is machine quilted.

2 Using **square for binding**, follow **Binding**, page 248, to bind wall hanging using 2¹/₂"w bias binding with mitered corners.

Row A (make 2)

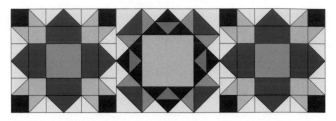

Row B

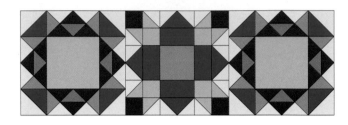

Quilt Diagram

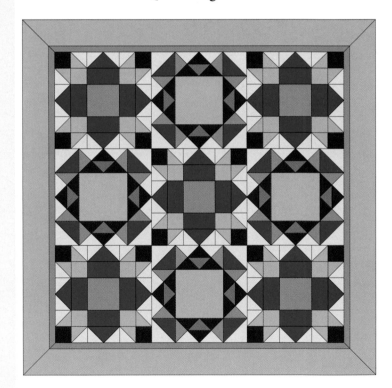

DYNAMIC DUO
OPTIONAL QUILT SIZES

Number of Blocks	Finished Width of Mitered Borders*	Borders to Make*	Size of Blocks and Borders
3 x 3	4"	4 (4½" x 48")	44" x 44"
3 x 5	4"	2 (4½" x 48") 2 (4½" 72")	44" x 68"
5 x 5	4"	4 (4½" x 72")	68" x 68"
5 x 7	4"	2 (4½" x 72") 2 (4 ½" x 96")	68" x 92"
5 x 7	6"	2(6½" x 76") 2(6½" x 100")	72" x 96"
7 x 7	6"	4(6½" x 100")	96" x 96"
7 x 7	8"	4 (8½" x 104")	100" x 100"
7 x 9	8"	2 (8½" x 104") 2 (8½" x 128")	100" x 124"

Width may include one or more border strips. Sew border strips together before adding to quilt top.

Sizes of mattress tops:

Crib: 27" x 52"

Twin: 39" x 75"

Full: 54" x 75"

Queen: 60" x 80"

King 76" x 80"

To determine **width** of quilt for your bed, add the width of mattress top and twice the depth of mattress–or depth you wish quilt to hang from bed top. To determine **length** of quilt, add the length of mattress top and depth of mattress or depth you wish quilt to hang at foot-of-bed. Add extra to length for pillow tuck, if desired.

DYNAMIC DUO

Magic Triangles, page 116, and
Crow's Foot, page 52

Arrow Star, page 4, and
Pinwheel, page 148

Robbing Peter to Pay Paul, page 164, and
Bright Stars, page 16

Capital T, page 20, and
Mrs. Bryan's Choice, page 128

Flutter Wheel, page 76, and
Checkerboard, page 36

Hen and Chicks, page 96, and
Memory, page 124

Navajo, page 132, and
Jacob's Ladder, page 100

Dove-in-the-Window, page 64, and
Boxes, page 12

DYNAMIC DUO

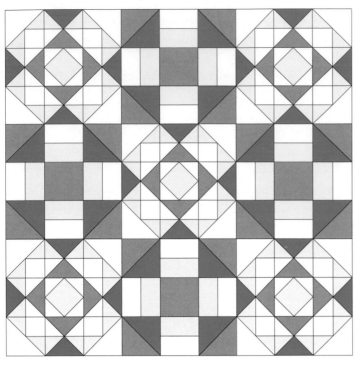

Boxes, page 12, and
Churn Dash, page 40

Dove-in-the-Window, page 64, and
Capital T, page 20

Dublin Steps, page 68, and
Swamp Angel, page 188

Maple Leaf, page 120, and
Pinwheel Askew, page 156

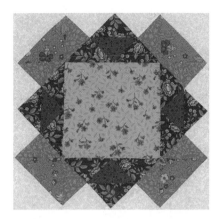

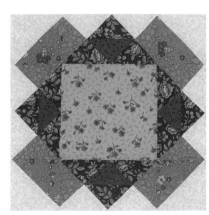

Attaching a hanging sleeve to the back of your wall hanging or quilt before the binding is added allows your project to be displayed on the wall.

1 Measure width of quilt top edge and subtract 1". Cut piece of fabric 7"w by determined measurement.

2 Press short edges of fabric piece $1/4$" to wrong side; press edges $1/4$" to wrong side again and machine stitch in place.

3 Matching wrong sides, fold piece in half lengthwise to form tube.

4 Follow project instructions or **General Instructions** to sew binding to quilt top and to trim backing and batting. Before blindstitching binding to backing, match raw edges and stitch hanging sleeve to center top edge on back of quilt.

5 Finish binding quilt, treating hanging sleeve as part of backing.

6 Blindstitch bottom of hanging sleeve to backing, taking care not to stitch through to front of quilt.

TERRIFIC TABLE RUNNER

Dress up any table with this *Terrific Table Runner*. If you love decorating for the seasons, make a different one for every holiday!

Finished Size: 43" x 19" (109 cm x 48 cm)

*Our table runner uses 3 **Laurel Wreath Blocks** (page 108). Use your choice of **block** or combination of **blocks**. We offer a few suggestions on page 221. The chart on page 221 provides information for making different length table runners.*

YARDAGE REQUIREMENTS

Note: *Substitute cream, rust, and green prints for the tan, light green, and dark green prints, respectively, listed in **Laurel Wreath Block** instructions. Yardages are based on our choice of **block**.*

- $5/8$ yd (57 cm) of cream print fabric*
- $3/8$ yd (34 cm) of tan and cream print fabric*
- $7/8$ yd (80 cm) of green print fabric*
- $1/8$ yd (11 cm) of rust print fabric*
- $1^1/2$ yds (1.4 m) for backing
- 51" x 27" (130 cm x 69 cm) piece of batting

CUTTING OUT THE BORDERS AND BINDING

From tan and cream print fabric:
- Cut 2 **long side outer borders** 3" x $37^1/2$".
- Cut 2 **short side outer borders** 3" x $13^1/2$".

From green print fabric:
- Cut 2 **long side inner borders** 1" x $37^1/2$".
- Cut 2 **short side inner borders** 1" x $12^1/2$".
- Cut **square for binding** 20" x 20".

From rust print fabric:
- Cut 4 **border corner squares** 3" x 3".

ASSEMBLING THE TABLE RUNNER

Use ¹/₄" seam allowances throughout.

1 Sew 3 **Laurel Wreath Blocks** together to make center section of table runner.

2 Sew 1 **border corner square** to each end of each **long side outer border**.

3 Sew **short side inner borders**, then **long side inner borders** to center section. Repeat to **add outer borders** to complete table runner top.

COMPLETING THE TABLE RUNNER

1 Following **Quilting**, page 243, to mark, layer, and quilt as desired. Our table runner is machine quilted.

2 Using **square for binding**, follow **Binding**, page 248, to bind table runner using 2¹/₂"w bias binding with mitered corners.

Table Runner Diagram

Using novelty prints or traditional colors, you can change your table runner for every holiday! Try using shamrock prints and **Dublin Steps Blocks**, page 68, to make a St. Patrick's Day table runner, or warm autumn colors and **Maple Leaf Blocks**, page 120, for Thanksgiving.

Remember our Veterans with **Memory Blocks,** *page 124, made in red, white, and blue for Memorial Day.*

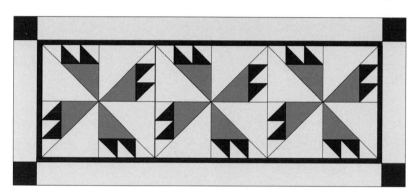

What's more perfect than **Rosebud Blocks,** *page 172, in reds and pinks for Valentine's Day?*

TABLE RUNNER
OPTIONAL LENGTHS

Number of Blocks	Cut Inner Borders	Cut Outer Borders	Finished Size
4	2 (1" x 49$^{1}/_{2}$") 2 (1" x 12$^{1}/_{2}$")	2 (3" x 49$^{1}/_{2}$")* 2 (3" x 13$^{1}/_{2}$")	55" x 19"
5	2 (1" x 61$^{1}/_{2}$") 2 (1" x 12$^{1}/_{2}$")	2 (3" x 61$^{1}/_{2}$")* 2 (3" x 13$^{1}/_{2}$")	67" x 19"
6	2 (1" x 73$^{1}/_{2}$") 2 (1" x 12$^{1}/_{2}$")	2 (3" x 73$^{1}/_{2}$")* 2 (3" x 13$^{1}/_{2}$")	79" x 19"

*Add **border squares** to **long side outer borders** before sewing to table runner.*

TERRIFIC TABLE RUNNER

PERFECT PILLOW

Memory Block is featured in our 12" pillow with matching welting. Imagine your bed or couch covered with all sizes and colors of beautiful pillows and shams!

Finished Size: 12" x 12" (30 cm x 30 cm)

*Our pillow is made using **Memory Block**, page 124. The pillow top is not quilted, and the edges are finished with welting. You may use any block to make a throw pillow like the one here, or any of the pillows and shams on pages 224 – 231.*

YARDAGE REQUIREMENTS
*(Based on our choice of **block**.)*
- $^1/_8$ yd (11 cm) of cream print fabric
- $^1/_4$ yd (23 cm) of burgundy print
- $^7/_8$ yd (80 cm) of teal print fabric
- Scrap of gold print fabric

You will also need:
- 12" x 12" (30.5 cm x 30.5 cm) pillow form
- $1^1/_2$ yds (1.4 m) of $^3/_8$" (9.5 mm) diameter cord

CUTTING OUT THE BACKING AND CORDING FABRIC
From teal print fabric:
- Cut 2 **pillow back pieces** $7^3/_4$" x $12^1/_2$".
- Cut **bias strip for welting** 3" x 54", piecing as necessary.

ASSEMBLING THE PILLOW

Use ¹/₄" seam allowances throughout.

1 Follow **Adding Welting and Ruffles to Pillows,** page 253, to sew welting to your **block.**

2 On each **pillow back piece**, press 1 long edge ¹/₄" to the wrong side; press ¹/₄" to the wrong side again and stitch in place.

3 Overlap hemmed edges of pillow back pieces, right sides facing up, to form 12¹/₂" x 12¹/₂" square. Baste pillow back pieces together at overlap.

4 Pin pillow top and pillow back together, right sides facing; stitch front and back together. Remove basting from pillow back, turn, and press. Insert pillow form.

12" x 12" Pillow Diagram

PERFECT PILLOW

*You may make your pillows and shams with or without quilting. If you choose not to quilt your shams, we recommend lining the sham tops with fleece to give extra body to the flanges. If you choose to quilt your pillow or sham, follow **Quilting**, page 243, to mark, layer, and quilt pillow top before adding welting, ruffle, or back to pillow.*

14" X 14" PILLOW

(36 cm x 36 cm)

Use $1/4$" seam allowances throughout.

1 Cut 2 **pillow back pieces** $8^3/4$" x $14^1/2$"; 2 **side borders** $1^1/2$" x $12^1/2$", and 2 **top/bottom borders** $1^1/2$" x $14^1/2$".

2 Add **side**, **top**, then **bottom borders** to **block** to finish pillow top.

3 Refer to **Adding Welting and Ruffles to Pillows**, page 253, if you wish to add welting or ruffle. Follow Steps 2 - 4 of **Assembling the Pillow**, page 223, to make pillow, except in Step 3 you will need to form a $14^1/2$" x $14^1/2$" square for pillow back.

16" X 16" PILLOW

(41 cm x 41 cm)

Use $1/4$" seam allowances throughout.

1 Cut 2 **pillow back pieces** $9^3/4$" x $16^1/2$"; 4 **borders** $2^1/2$" x $12^1/2$", and 4 **border corner squares** $2^1/2$" x $2^1/2$".

2 Sew 1 **border corner square** to each end of 2 **borders** to make **top** and **bottom borders**. Add **side**, **top**, then **bottom borders** to **block** to complete pillow top.

3 Refer to **Adding Welting and Ruffles to Pillows**, page 253, if you wish to add welting or ruffle. Follow Steps 2 – 4 of **Assembling the Pillow**, page 223, to make pillow, except in Step 3 you will need to form a $16^1/2$" x $16^1/2$" square for pillow back.

14" x 14" Pillow Diagram

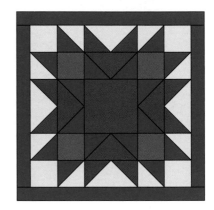

16" x 16" Pillow Diagram

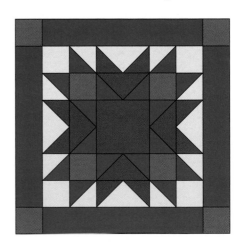

18" X 18" PILLOW
(46 cm x 46 cm)

Use ¹/₄" seam allowances throughout.

1 Cut 2 **pillow back pieces** 11¹/₄" x 18¹/₂"; 4 **inner border strips** 1¹/₂" x 22¹/₂", and 4 **outer border strips** 2¹/₂" x 22¹/₂".

2 Sew 1 **inner border strip** and 1 **outer border strip** together lengthwise to make 1 **border**. Make 4 **borders**. Following **Adding Mitered Borders**, page 240, add borders to **block** to complete pillow top.

3 Refer to **Adding Welting and Ruffles to Pillows**, page 253, if you wish to add welting or ruffle. Follow Steps 2 - 4 of **Assembling the Pillow**, page 223, to make pillow, except in Step 3 you will need to form an 18¹/₂" x 18¹/₂" square for pillow back.

18" x 18" Pillow Diagram

20" X 20" PILLOW
(51 cm x 51 cm)

Use ¹/₄" seam allowances throughout.

1 Cut 2 **pillow back pieces** 12¹/₄" x 20¹/₂", 2 squares 9³/₈" x 9³/₈" cut *once* diagonally to make 4 **setting triangles**, 2 **side borders** 2" x 17¹/₂", and 2 **top/bottom borders** 2" x 20¹/₂".

2 Referring to **20" x 20" Pillow Diagram**, sew **setting triangles** to **block**.

3 Sew **side**, **top**, then **bottom borders** to complete pillow top.

4 Refer to **Adding Welting and Ruffles to Pillows**, page 253, if you wish to add welting or ruffle. Follow Steps 2 - 4 of **Assembling the Pillow**, page 223, to make pillow, except in Step 3 you will need to form a 20¹/₂" x 20¹/₂" square for pillow back.

20" x 20" Pillow Diagram

PERFECT PILLOW

24" X 24" PILLOW
(61 cm x 61 cm)

Use ¹/₄" seam allowances throughout. You will need 4 blocks.

1 Cut 2 **pillow back pieces** 14¹/₄" x 24¹/₂".

2 Sew 4 **blocks** together. (*Mix and match blocks if you wish.*)

3 Refer to **Adding Welting and Ruffles to Pillows**, page 253, if you wish to add welting or ruffle. Follow Steps 2 - 4 of **Assembling the Pillow**, page 223, to make pillow, except in Step 3 you will need to form a 24¹/₂" x 24¹/₂" square for pillow back.

STANDARD-SIZE PILLOW SHAM #1
Finished size: 30" x 24" (76 cm x 61 cm)

Fits a standard-size 26" x 20" (66 cm x 51 cm) pillow. Use ¹/₄" seam allowances except where indicated otherwise. You will need 2 blocks.

1 Cut 2 **pillow sham back pieces** 17¹/₂" x 25", 2 **side borders** 3³/₄" x 12¹/₂", and 2 **top/bottom borders** 6³/₄" x 31".

2 Referring to **Standard-Size Pillow Sham Diagram #1**, sew 2 **blocks** together.

3 Sew **side**, **top**, then **bottom borders** to complete pillow sham top.

4 On each **pillow sham back piece**, press 1 long edge ¹/₄" to the wrong side; press ¹/₄" to the wrong side again and stitch in place.

5 Overlap hemmed edges of **pillow sham back pieces**, right sides facing up, to form 31" x 25" rectangle. Baste pillow back pieces together at overlap.

24" x 24" Pillow Diagram

Standard-Size Pillow Sham #1 Diagram

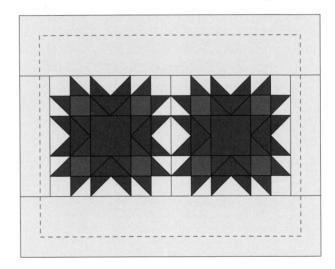

6 Pin pillow sham top and pillow sham back together, right sides facing. **Using ¹/₂" seam allowance**, stitch front and back together. Remove basting from pillow sham back, turn, and press.

7 Top stitch through all layers 2" from edges to form 2" flange on all sides as shown by dashed line in diagram.

STANDARD-SIZE PILLOW SHAM #2
Finished size: 30" x 24" (76 cm x 61 cm)

*Fits a standard-size 26" x 20" (66 cm x 51 cm) pillow. Use ¹/₄" seam allowances except where indicated otherwise. You will need 1 **block**.*

1 Cut 2 **pillow sham back pieces** 17¹/₂" x 25", 2 squares 9³/₈" x 9³/₈" cut *once* diagonally to make 4 **setting triangles**, 2 **side borders** 7¹/₄" x 17¹/₂", and 2 **top/bottom borders** 4¹/₄" x 31".

2 Referring to **Standard-Size Pillow Sham Diagram #2**, sew **setting triangles** to **block**.

3 Sew **side**, **top**, then **bottom borders** to complete pillow sham top.

4 Repeat Steps 4 - 7 of **Standard-Size Pillow Sham #1**, page 226, to complete sham.

Standard-Size Pillow Sham #2 Diagram

QUEEN-SIZE PILLOW SHAM #1
Finished size: 34" x 24" (86 cm x 61 cm)

*Fits a queen-size 30" x 20" (76 cm x 51 cm) pillow. Use ¹/₄" seam allowances except where indicated otherwise. You will need 2 **blocks**.*

1 Cut 2 **pillow sham back pieces** 19¹/₂" x 25", 2 **side borders** 5³/₄" x 12¹/₂", and 2 **top/bottom borders** 6³/₄" x 35".

2 Referring to **Queen-Size Pillow Sham #1 Diagram**, sew 2 **blocks** together.

3 Sew **side**, **top**, then **bottom borders** to complete pillow sham top.

Queen-Size Pillow Sham #1 Diagram

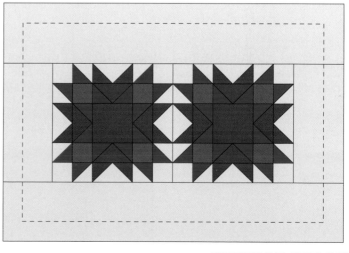

PERFECT PILLOW

4 On each **pillow sham back piece**, press 1 long edge $^1/_4$" to the wrong side; press $^1/_4$" to the wrong side again and stitch in place.

5 Overlap hemmed edges of **pillow sham back pieces**, right sides facing up, to form 35" x 25" rectangle. Baste pillow back pieces together at overlap.

6 Pin pillow sham top and pillow sham back together, right sides facing. **Using $^1/_2$" seam allowance**, stitch front and back together. Remove basting from pillow sham back, turn, and press.

7 Top stitch through all layers 2" from edges to form 2" flange on all sides as shown by dashed line in diagram.

QUEEN-SIZE PILLOW SHAM #2
Finished size: 34" x 24" (86 cm x 61 cm)
*Fits a queen-size 30" x 20" (76 cm x 51 cm) pillow. Use $^1/_4$" seam allowances except where indicated otherwise. You will need 1 **block**.*

1 Cut 2 **pillow sham back pieces** 19$^1/_2$" x 25", 2 squares 9$^3/_8$" x 9$^3/_8$" cut *once* diagonally to make 4 **setting triangles**, 2 **side borders** 9$^1/_4$" x 17$^1/_2$", and 2 **top/bottom borders** 4$^1/_4$" x 35".

2 Referring to **Queen-Size Pillow Sham #2 Diagram**, sew **setting triangles** to **block**.

3 Sew **side**, **top**, then **bottom borders** to complete pillow sham top.

4 Follow Steps 4 - 7 of **Queen-Size Pillow Sham #1**, page 227, to complete sham.

Queen-Size Pillow Sham #2 Diagram

KING-SIZE PILLOW SHAM #1

Finished size: 40" x 24" (102 cm x 61 cm)

Fits a king-size 36" x 20" (91 cm x 51 cm) pillow. Use ¹/₄" seam allowances except where indicated otherwise. You will need 3 blocks.

1 Cut 2 **pillow sham back pieces** 22¹/₂" x 25", 2 **side borders** 2³/₄" x 12¹/₂", and 2 **top/bottom borders** 6³/₄" x 41".

2 Referring to **King-Size Pillow Sham #1 Diagram**, sew 3 **blocks** together.

3 Sew **side**, **top**, then **bottom borders** to complete pillow sham top.

4 On each **pillow sham back piece**, press 1 long edge ¹/₄" to the wrong side; press ¹/₄" to the wrong side again and stitch in place.

5 Overlap hemmed edges of **pillow sham back pieces**, right sides facing up, to form 41" x 25" rectangle. Baste pillow back pieces together at overlap.

6 Pin pillow sham top and pillow sham back together, right sides facing. **Using ¹/₂" seam allowance**, stitch front and back together. Remove basting from pillow sham back, turn, and press.

7 Top stitch through all layers 2" from edges to form 2" flange on all sides as shown by dashed line in diagram.

King-Size Pillow Sham #1 Diagram

PERFECT PILLOW

KING-SIZE PILLOW SHAM #2

Finished size: 40" x 24" (102 cm x 61 cm)

*Fits a king-size 36" x 20" (91 cm x 51 cm) pillow. Use ¹/₄" seam allowances except where indicated otherwise. You will need 2 **blocks**.*

1 Cut 2 **pillow sham back pieces** 17¹/₂" x 25", 2 squares 9³/₈" x 9³/₈" cut *once* diagonally to make 4 **small setting triangles**, 1 square 18¹/₄" x 18¹/₄" cut *twice* diagonally to make 4 **large setting triangles** (you will use 2 and have 2 left over), 2 **side borders** 3³/₄" x 17¹/₂", and 2 **top/bottom borders** 4¹/₄" x 41".

2 Referring to **King-Size Pillow Sham #2 Assembly Diagram**, sew **blocks**, small **setting triangles, and large setting triangles** together to make center section of sham top.

3 Sew **side**, **top**, then **bottom borders** to complete pillow sham top.

4 Follow Steps 4 - 7 of **King-Size Pillow Sham #1**, page 229, to complete sham.

EUROPEAN-SIZE PILLOW SHAM #1

Finished size: 30" x 30" (76 cm x 76 cm)

*Fits a European-size 26" x 26" (66 cm x 66 cm) pillow. Use ¹/₄" seam allowances except where indicated otherwise. You will need 4 **blocks**.*

1 Cut 2 **pillow sham back pieces** 18" x 31", 2 **side borders** 3³/₄" x 24¹/₂", and 2 **top/bottom borders** 3³/₄" x 31".

2 Referring to **European-Size Pillow Sham #1 Diagram**, page 231, sew 4 **blocks** together.

3 Sew **side**, **top**, then **bottom borders** to complete pillow sham top.

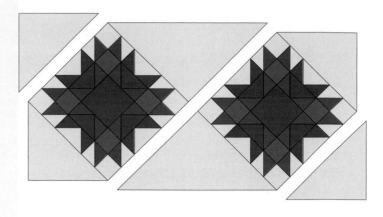

King-Size Pillow Sham #2 Assembly Diagram

King-Size Pillow Sham #2 Diagram

4 On each **pillow sham back piece**, press 1 long edge $1/4$" to the wrong side; press $1/4$" to the wrong side again and stitch in place.

5 Overlap hemmed edges of **pillow sham back pieces**, right sides facing up, to form 31" x 31" rectangle. Baste pillow back pieces together at overlap.

6 Pin pillow sham top and pillow sham back together, right sides facing. **Using $1/2$" seam allowance**, stitch front and back together. Remove basting from pillow sham back, turn, and press.

7 Top stitch through all layers 2" from edges to form 2" flange on all sides as shown by dashed line in diagram.

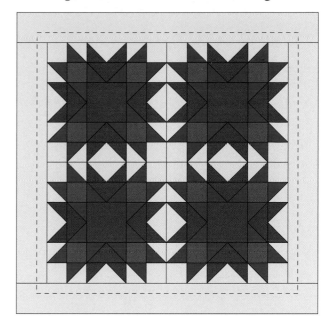

EUROPEAN-SIZE PILLOW SHAM #2

Finished size: 30" x 30" (76 cm x 76 cm)

*Fits a European-size 26" x 26" (66 cm x 66 cm) pillow. Use $1/4$" seam allowances except where indicated otherwise. You will need 1 **block**.*

1 Cut 2 **pillow sham back pieces** 21" x 31", 2 squares $9^{3}/8$" x $9^{3}/8$" cut *once* diagonally to make 4 **setting triangles**, 2 **side borders** $7^{1}/4$" x $17^{1}/2$", and 2 **top/bottom borders** $7^{1}/4$" x 31".

2 Referring to **European-Size Pillow Sham Diagram #2**, sew **setting triangles** to block.

3 Sew **side**, **top**, then **bottom borders** to complete pillow sham top.

4 Follow Steps 4 - 7 of **European-Size Pillow Sham #1** to complete sham.

European-Size Pillow Sham #2 Diagram

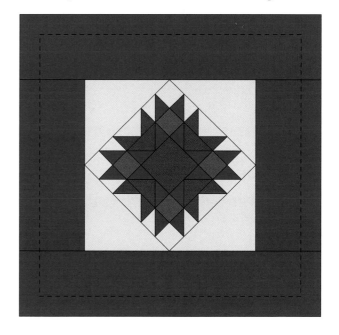

PERFECT PILLOW

PRETTY POINTS

Blocks *"turned on point"* add a special interest that many quilters love. To turn your **blocks** on point, resulting in diamonds, you will need to add **setting triangles**.

The table on page 233 provides various size quilts and lists the number of **setting triangles** and **setting corner triangles** needed for the number of **blocks** you use.

Sew **blocks** and **settings** in diagonal **rows** as shown in the **Turned on Point Diagrams**, then sew **rows** together.

After sewing **blocks** and **settings**, refer to **Borders**, page 240, if you wish to add borders. Follow **Quilting**, page 243, to mark, layer, and quilt as desired. Follow **Binding**, page 248, to finish your quilt.

Turned on Point Assembly Diagram

Turned on Point Quilt Top Diagram

BLOCKS TURNED ON POINT

Blocks Across x Down	Number of Blocks Needed	Number of Setting Corner Triangles**	Number of Setting Triangles***	Size of Blocks and Settings
1 x 1	1	4	0	17" x 17"
1 x 2	2	4	2	17" x 34"
1 x 3	3	4	4	17" x 51"
2 x 2	5	4	4	34" x 34"
2 x 3	8	4	6	34" x 51"
2 x 4	11	4	8	34" x 68"
3 x 3	13	4	8	51" x 51"
3 x 4	18	4	10	51" x 68"
3 x 5	23	4	12	51" x 85"
4 x 4	25	4	12	68" x 68"
4 x 5	32	4	14	68" x 85"
4 x 6	39	4	16	68" x 102"
5 x 6	50	4	18	85" x 102"
6 x 6	61	4	20	102" x 102"

Cut 2 squares $9^3/8$" x $9^3/8$". Cut squares **once diagonally to make 4 **corner setting triangles**.
***Cut squares $18^1/4$" x $18^1/4$". Cut each square **twice** diagonally to make 4 **setting triangles**.

Sizes of mattress tops:

Crib: 27" x 52"

Twin: 39" x 75"

Full: 54" x 75"

Queen: 60" x 80"

King 76" x 80"

To determine **width** of quilt for your bed, add the width of mattress top and twice the depth of mattress–or depth you wish quilt to hang from bed top. To determine **length** of quilt, add the length of mattress top and depth of mattress or depth you wish quilt to hang at foot-of-bed. Add extra to length for pillow tuck, if desired.

PRETTY POINTS

Alternating **blocks** with **setting squares** creates a completely different look and requires fewer **blocks**.

The table on page 235 provides various size quilts and lists the number of **setting triangles** and **setting corner triangles**, <u>plus</u> number of **setting squares** needed for the number of **blocks** you use.

Sew **blocks** and **settings** in diagonal **rows** as shown in the **Turned on Point Diagrams**, then sew **rows** together.

After sewing **blocks** and **settings**, refer to **Borders**, page 240, if you wish to add borders. Follow **Quilting**, page 243, to mark, layer, and quilt as desired. Follow **Binding**, page 248, to finish your quilt.

Turned on Point Assembly Diagram
(With Setting Squares)

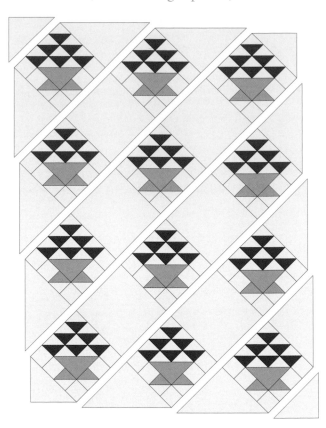

Turned on Point Quilt Top Diagram
(With Setting Squares)

BLOCKS TURNED ON POINT
SIZES OF QUILTS WITH SETTING SQUARES

Blocks Across x Down	Number of Blocks	Number of Setting Squares*	Number of Setting Corner Triangles**	Number of Setting Triangles***	Size of Blocks and Settings
2 x 2	4	1	4	4	34" x 34"
2 x 3	6	2	4	6	34" x 51"
2 x 4	8	3	4	8	34" x 68"
3 x 3	9	4	4	8	51" x 51"
3 x 4	12	6	4	10	51" x 68"
3 x 5	15	8	4	12	51" x 85"
4 x 4	16	9	4	12	68" x 68"
4 x 5	20	12	4	14	68" x 85"
4 x 6	24	15	4	16	68" x 102"
5 x 6	30	20	4	18	85" x 102"
6 x 6	36	25	4	20	102" x 102"

*Cut **setting squares** $12^{1}/_{2}$" x $12^{1}/_{2}$".
Cut 2 squares $9^{3}/_{8}$" x $9^{3}/_{8}$". Cut squares **once diagonally to make 4 **corner setting triangles**.
***Cut squares $18^{1}/_{4}$" x $18^{1}/_{4}$". Cut each square **twice** diagonally to make 4 **setting triangles**.

Sizes of mattress tops:

Crib: 27" x 52"

Twin: 39" x 75"

Full: 54" x 75"

Queen: 60" x 80"

King 76" x 80"

To determine **width** of quilt for your bed, add the width of mattress top and twice the depth of mattress–or depth you wish quilt to hang from bed top. To determine **length** of quilt, add the length of mattress top and depth of mattress or depth you wish quilt to hang at foot-of-bed. Add extra to length for pillow tuck, if desired.

GENERAL INSTRUCTIONS

To make your quilting easier and more enjoyable, we encourage you to carefully read all of the general instructions, study the color photographs, and familiarize yourself with the individual project instructions before beginning a project.

SELECTING FABRICS

Choose high-quality, medium-weight 100% cotton fabrics. All-cotton fabrics hold a crease better, fray less, and are easier to quilt than cotton/polyester blends.

Yardage requirements listed for each project are based on 45" wide fabric with a "usable" width of 42" after shrinkage and trimming selvages. Actual usable width will probably vary slightly from fabric to fabric. Our recommended yardage lengths should be adequate for occasional resquaring of fabric when many cuts are required.

PREPARING FABRICS

We recommend that all fabrics be washed, dried, and pressed before cutting. If fabrics are not pre-washed, washing finished quilt will cause shrinkage and give it a more "antiqued" look and feel. Bright and dark colors, which may run, should always be washed before cutting. After washing and drying fabric, fold lengthwise with wrong sides together and matching selvages.

ROTARY CUTTING

Rotary cutting has brought speed and accuracy to quiltmaking by allowing quilters to easily cut strips of fabric and then cut those strips into smaller pieces.

- Place fabric on work surface with fold closest to you.

- Cut all strips from selvage-to-selvage width of fabric unless otherwise indicated in project instructions.

- Square left edge of fabric using rotary cutter and rulers or ruler and triangle (**Figs. 1- 2**).

- To cut each strip required for a project, place ruler over cut edge of fabric, aligning desired marking on ruler with cut edge; make cut (**Fig. 3**).

- When cutting several strips from a single piece of fabric, it is important to make sure that cuts remain at a perfect right angle to the fold; square fabric as needed.

Fig. 1

Fig. 2

Fig. 3

237

Precise cutting, followed by accurate piecing, will ensure that all pieces of quilt top fit together well.

HAND PIECING

- Use ruler and sharp fabric marking pencil to draw all seam lines onto back of cut pieces.

- Matching right sides, pin 2 pieces together, using pins to mark corners (**Fig. 4**).

- Use Running Stitch to sew pieces together along drawn line, backstitching at beginning and end of seam. Do not extend stitches into seam allowances (**Fig. 5**).

- Run 5 or 6 stitches onto needle before pulling needle through fabric.

- To add stability, backstitch every $^3/_4$" to 1".

MACHINE PIECING

- Set sewing machine stitch length for approximately 11 stitches per inch.

- Use neutral-colored general-purpose sewing thread (not quilting thread) in needle and in bobbin.

- An accurate $^1/_4$" seam allowance is *essential.* Even a slight discrepancy will make a difference in finished block size, especially those blocks with many pieces. Presser feet that are $^1/_4$" wide are available for most sewing machines.

- When piecing, always place pieces right sides together and match raw edges; pin if necessary.

- Chain piecing (**Fig. 6**) saves time and will usually result in more accurate piecing.

- Trim away points of seam allowances that extend beyond edges of sewn pieces (**Fig. 7**).

Fig. 4

Fig. 5

Fig. 6

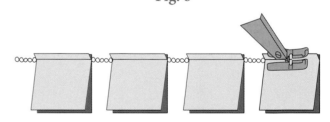

Fig. 7

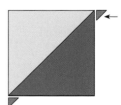

Sewing Across Seam Intersections

When sewing across intersection of 2 seams, place pieces right sides together and match seams exactly, making sure seam allowances are pressed in opposite directions (**Fig. 8**).

Sewing Sharp Points

To ensure sharp points when joining triangular or diagonal pieces, stitch across the center of the "X" (shown in red) formed on wrong side by previous seams (**Fig. 9**).

PRESSING

- Use steam iron set on "Cotton" for all pressing.

- Press after sewing each seam.

- Seam allowances are almost always pressed to 1 side, usually toward darker fabric. However, to reduce bulk it may occasionally be necessary to press seam allowances toward the lighter fabric or even to press them open.

- To prevent dark fabric seam allowance from showing through light fabric, trim darker seam allowance slightly narrower than lighter seam allowance.

- To press long seams, such as those in long strip sets, without curving or other distortion, lay strips across width of the ironing board.

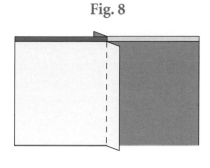

Fig. 8

Fig. 9

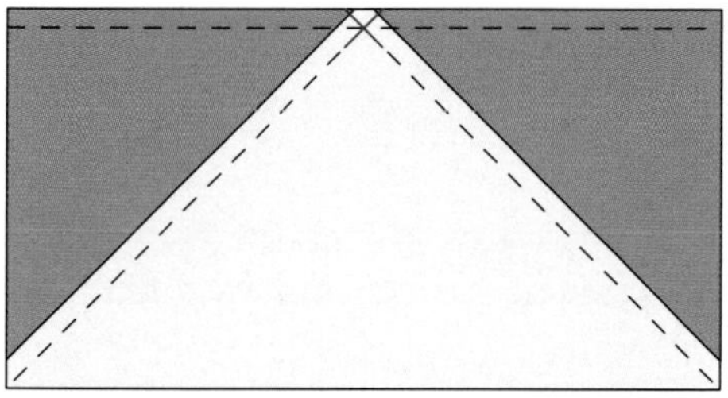

GENERAL INSTRUCTIONS

Borders cut along the lengthwise grain will lie flatter than borders cut along the crosswise grain. If cutting borders before finishing center section of quilt, we recommend adding 2" of length at each end for "insurance" and trimming borders after measuring completed center section of quilt top.

ADDING SQUARED BORDERS

1 Mark the center of each edge of quilt top.

2 Squared borders are usually added to side, then top and bottom edges of the center section of a quilt top. To add side borders, measure across center of quilt top to determine length of borders (**Fig. 10**). Trim side borders to the determined length.

3 Mark center of 1 long edge of side border. Matching center marks and raw edges, pin border to quilt top, easing in any fullness; stitch. Repeat for other side border.

4 Measure center of quilt top, including attached borders, to determine length of top and bottom borders. Trim top and bottom borders to the determined length. Repeat Step 3 to add borders to quilt top (**Fig. 11**).

ADDING MITERED BORDERS

Mitered borders may consist of 1 or more fabric strips. Strips should be cut the same length for each side of quilt and sewn together before adding to quilt top. If mitered border measurements are provided in project, skip to Step 2.

1 Measure across center of quilt to determine height and width (**Fig. 12**). Add *length* of quilt, plus double the width of desired borders, plus 4" to determine length of top and bottom borders to cut. Add *width* of quilt, plus double the finished width of desired borders, plus 4" to determine length of side borders to cut.

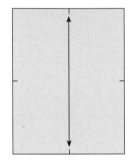

Fig. 10

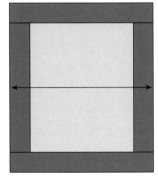

Fig. 11

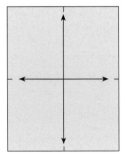

Fig. 12

2 Mark the center of each edge of quilt top.

3 Mark center of 1 long edge of top border. Measure across center of quilt top. Matching center marks and raw edges, pin border to center of quilt top edge. Beginning at center of border, measure $\frac{1}{2}$ the width of the quilt top in both directions and mark. Match marks on border with corners of quilt top and pin. Easing in any fullness, pin border to quilt top between center and corners. Sew border to quilt top, beginning and ending seams *exactly* $\frac{1}{4}$" from each corner of quilt top and backstitching at beginning and end of stitching (**Fig. 13**).

4 Repeat Step 3 to sew bottom, then side borders to center section of quilt top. To temporarily move first 2 borders out of the way, fold and pin ends as shown in **Fig 14**.

5 Fold 1 corner of quilt top diagonally with right sides together and matching edges. Use ruler to mark stitching line as shown in **Fig. 15**. Pin borders together along drawn line. Sew on drawn line, backstitching at beginning and end of stitching (**Fig. 16**).

6 Turn mitered corner right side up. Check to make sure corner will lie flat with no gaps or puckers.

7 Trim seam allowance to $\frac{1}{4}$"; press to 1 side.

8 Repeat Steps 5 - 7 to miter each remaining corner.

Fig. 13

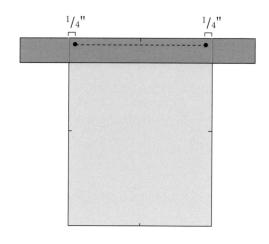

Fig. 14

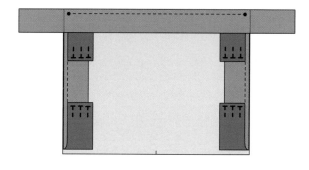

Fig. 15

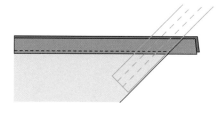

Fig. 16

GENERAL INSTRUCTIONS

TYPES OF QUILTING DESIGNS

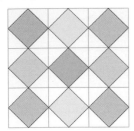

In the Ditch Quilting
Quilting along seamlines or along edges of appliquéd pieces is called "in the ditch" quilting. This type of quilting should be done on side **opposite** seam allowance and does not have to be marked.

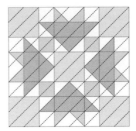

Channel Quilting
Quilting with straight, parallel lines is called "channel" quilting. This type of quilting may be marked or stitched using a guide.

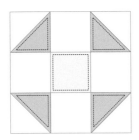

Outline Quilting
Quilting a consistent distance, usually $1/4$", from seam or appliqué is called "outline" quilting. Outline quilting may be marked, or $1/4$" masking tape may be placed along seamlines for quilting guide. (Do not leave tape on quilt longer than necessary, since it may leave an adhesive residue.)

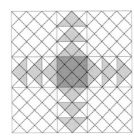

Crosshatch Quilting
Quilting straight lines in a grid pattern is called "crosshatch" quilting. Lines may be stitched parallel to edges of quilt or stitched diagonally. This type of quilting may be marked or stitched using a guide.

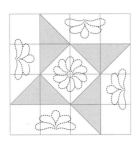

Motif Quilting
Quilting a design, such as a feathered wreath, is called "motif" quilting. This type of quilting should be marked before basting quilt layers together.

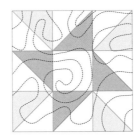

Meandering Quilting
Quilting in random curved lines and swirls is called "meandering" quilting. Quilting lines should not cross or touch each other. This type of quilting does not need to be marked.

Echo Quilting
Quilting that follows the outline of an appliquéd or pieced design with 2 or more parallel lines is called "echo" quilting. This type of quilting does not need to be marked.

Stipple Quilting
Meandering quilting that is very closely spaced is called "stipple" quilting. Stippling will flatten the area quilted and is often stitched in background areas to raise appliquéd or pieced designs. This type of quilting does not need to be marked.

Quilting holds the 3 layers (top, batting, and backing) of the quilt together and can be done by hand or machine. Because marking, layering, and quilting are interrelated and may be done in different orders depending on circumstances, please read entire **Quilting** *section before beginning project.*

MARKING QUILTING LINES

Quilting lines may be marked using fabric marking pencils, chalk markers, water or air soluble pens, or lead pencils.

Simple quilting designs may be marked with chalk or chalk pencil after basting. A small area may be marked, then quilted, before moving to next area to be marked. Intricate designs should be marked before basting using a more durable marker.

Caution: Some marks may be permanently set by pressing. **Test** different markers **on scrap fabric** to find one that marks clearly and can be thoroughly removed.

A wide variety of precut quilting stencils, as well as entire books of quilting patterns, are available. Using a stencil makes it easier to mark intricate or repetitive designs.

To make a stencil from a pattern, center template plastic over pattern and use a permanent marker to trace pattern onto plastic. Use a craft knife with single or double blade to cut channels along traced lines (**Fig. 17**).

Fig. 17

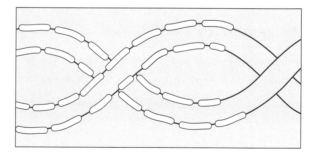

PREPARING THE BACKING

To allow for slight shifting of quilt top during quilting, backing should be approximately 4" larger on all sides. Yardage requirements listed for quilt backings are calculated for 45"w fabric. Using 90"w or 108"w fabric for the backing may eliminate piecing. To piece a backing using 45"w fabric, use the following instructions.

1 Measure length and width of quilt top; add 8" to each measurement.

2 If determined width is 84" or less, cut backing fabric into 2 lengths slightly longer than determined **length** measurement. Trim selvages. Place lengths with right sides facing and sew long edges together, forming tube (**Fig. 18**). Match seams and press along 1 fold (**Fig. 19**). Cut along pressed fold to form single piece (**Fig. 20**).

3 If determined width is more than 84", cut backing fabric into 3 lengths slightly longer than determined **width** measurement. Trim selvages. Sew long edges together to form single piece.

4 Trim backing to size determined in Step 1; press seam allowances open.

CHOOSING THE BATTING

The appropriate batting will make quilting easier. For fine hand quilting, choose low-loft batting. All cotton or cotton/polyester blend battings work well for machine quilting because the cotton helps "grip" quilt layers. If quilt is to be tied, a high-loft batting, sometimes called extra-loft or fat batting, may be used to make quilt "fluffy."

Types of batting include cotton, polyester, cotton/polyester blend, wool, cotton/wool blend, and silk.

When selecting batting, refer to package labels for characteristics and care instructions. Cut batting same size as prepared backing.

Fig. 18

Fig. 19

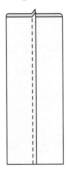

Fig. 20

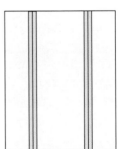

244

ASSEMBLING THE QUILT

1 Examine wrong side of quilt top closely; trim any seam allowances and clip any threads that may show through front of the quilt. Press quilt top, being careful not to "set" any marked quilting lines.

2 Place backing **wrong** side up on flat surface. Use masking tape to tape edges of backing to surface. Place batting on top of backing fabric. Smooth batting gently, being careful not to stretch or tear. Center quilt top **right** side up on batting.

3 If hand quilting, begin in center and work toward outer edges to hand baste all layers together. Use long stitches and place basting lines approximately 4" apart (**Fig. 21**). Smooth fullness or wrinkles toward outer edges.

4 If machine quilting, use 1" rustproof safety pins to "pin-baste" all layers together, spacing pins approximately 4" apart. Begin at center and work toward outer edges to secure all layers. If possible, place pins away from areas that will be quilted, although pins may be removed as needed when quilting.

HAND QUILTING

The quilting stitch is a basic running stitch that forms a broken line on quilt top and backing. Stitches on quilt top and backing should be straight and equal in length.

1 Secure center of quilt in hoop or frame. Check quilt top and backing to make sure they are smooth. To help prevent puckers, always begin quilting in the center of quilt and work toward outside edges.

2 Thread needle with 18" - 20" length of quilting thread; knot 1 end. Using thimble, insert needle into quilt top and batting approximately $1/2$" from quilting line. Bring needle up on quilting line (**Fig. 22**); when knot catches on quilt top, give thread a quick, short pull to "pop" knot through fabric into batting (**Fig. 23**).

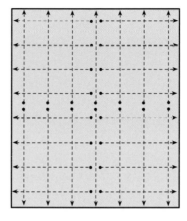

Fig. 21

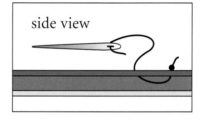

Fig. 22

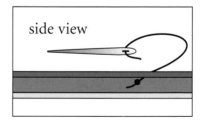

Fig. 23

GENERAL INSTRUCTIONS

3 Holding needle with sewing hand and placing other hand underneath quilt, use thimble to push tip of needle down through all layers. As soon as needle touches finger underneath, use that finger to push tip of needle only back up through layers to top of quilt. (The amount of needle showing above fabric determines length of quilting stitch.) Referring to **Fig. 24**, rock needle up and down, taking 3 - 6 stitches before bringing needle and thread completely through layers. Check back of quilt to make sure stitches are going through all layers. If necessary, make 1 stitch at a time when quilting through seam allowances or along curves and corners.

4 At end of thread, knot thread close to fabric and "pop" knot into batting; clip thread close to fabric.

5 Move hoop as often as necessary. Thread may be left dangling and picked up again after returning to that part of quilt.

MACHINE QUILTING METHODS

Use general-purpose thread in bobbin. Do not use quilting thread. Thread the needle of machine with general-purpose thread or transparent monofilament thread to make quilting blend with quilt top fabrics. Use decorative thread, such as a metallic or contrasting-color general-purpose thread, to make quilting lines stand out more.

Straight Line Quilting

The term "straight line" is somewhat deceptive, since curves (especially gentle ones) as well as straight lines can be stitched with this technique. See **Fig. 25** *for an example of straight line quilting.*

1 Set stitch length for 6 - 10 stitches per inch and attach walking foot to sewing machine.

2 Determine which section of quilt will have longest continuous quilting line, oftentimes area from center top to center bottom. Roll up and secure each edge of quilt to help reduce the bulk, keeping fabrics smooth. Smaller projects may not need to be rolled.

Fig. 24

Fig. 25

3 Begin stitching on longest quilting line, using very short stitches for the first $1/4$" to "lock" quilting. Stitch across project, using 1 hand on each side of walking foot to slightly spread fabric and to guide fabric through machine. Lock stitches at end of quilting line.

4 Continue machine quilting, stitching longer quilting lines first to stabilize quilt before moving on to other areas.

Free Motion Quilting

*Free motion quilting (**Fig. 26**) may be free form or may follow a marked pattern.*

1 Attach darning foot to sewing machine and lower or cover feed dogs.

2 Position quilt under darning foot. Holding top thread, take 1 stitch and pull bobbin thread to top of quilt. To "lock" beginning of quilting line, hold top and bobbin threads while making 3 to 5 stitches in place.

3 Use 1 hand on each side of darning foot to slightly spread fabric and to move fabric through the machine. Even stitch length is achieved by using smooth, flowing hand motion and steady machine speed. Slow machine speed and fast hand movement will create long stitches. Fast machine speed and slow hand movement will create short stitches. Move quilt sideways, back and forth, in a circular motion, or in a random motion to create desired designs; do not rotate quilt. Lock stitches at end of each quilting line.

Fig. 26

GENERAL INSTRUCTIONS

Binding encloses the raw edges of quilt. Because of its stretchiness, bias binding works well for binding projects with curves or rounded corners and tends to lie smooth and flat in any given circumstance. Binding may also be cut from straight lengthwise or crosswise grain of fabric.

MAKING CONTINUOUS BIAS STRIP BINDING

Bias strips for binding can simply be cut and pieced to desired length. However, when a long length of binding is needed, the "continuous" method is quick and accurate.

1 Cut square from binding fabric the size indicated in project instructions or refer to table at right for square size. Cut square in half diagonally to make 2 triangles.

2 With right sides together and using ¼" seam allowance, sew triangles together (**Fig. 27**); press seam allowance open.

SQUARE SIZE FOR BINDING

If distance around quilt top is *LESS THAN*	Cut square for binding
49"	13" x 13"
58"	14" x 14"
68"	15" x 15"
79"	16" x 16"
91"	17" x 17"
103"	18" x 18"
116"	19" x 19"
130"	20" x 20"
145"	21" x 21"
161"	22" x 22"
177"	23" x 23"
194"	24" x 24"
212"	25" x 25"
231"	26" x 26"
251"	27" x 27"
271"	28" x 28"
292"	29" x 29"
314"	30" x 30"
337"	31" x 31"
361"	32" x 32"
385"	33" x 33"
410"	34" x 34"
436"	35" x 35"

Fig. 27

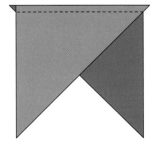

3 On wrong side of fabric, draw lines the width of binding as specified in project instructions, usually 2¹/₂" (**Fig. 28**). Cut off any remaining fabric less than this width.

4 With right sides inside, bring short edges together to form tube; match raw edges so that first drawn line of top section meets second drawn line of bottom section (**Fig. 29**).

5 Carefully pin edges together by inserting pins through drawn lines at point where drawn lines intersect, making sure pins go through intersections on both sides. Using ¹/₄" seam allowance, sew edges together; press seam allowance open.

6 To cut continuous strip, begin cutting along first drawn line (**Fig. 30**). Continue cutting along drawn line around tube.

7 Trim ends of bias strip square.

8 Matching wrong sides and raw edges, press bias strip in half lengthwise to complete binding.

Fig. 28

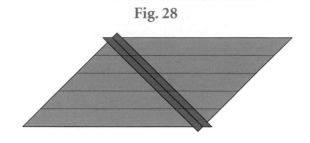

Fig. 29

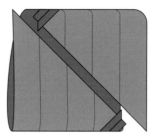

Fig. 30

GENERAL INSTRUCTIONS

MAKING STRAIGHT-GRAIN BINDING

1. To determine length of strip needed if attaching binding with mitered corners, measure edges of quilt and add 12".

2. Cut lengthwise or crosswise strips of binding fabric the determined length x the width called for in project instructions. Strips may be pieced to achieve necessary length.

3. Matching wrong sides and raw edges, press strip(s) in half lengthwise to complete binding.

ATTACHING BINDING WITH MITERED CORNERS

1. Beginning with 1 end near center on bottom edge of quilt, lay binding around quilt to make sure that seams in binding will not end up at a corner. Adjust placement if necessary. Matching raw edges of binding to raw edge of quilt top, pin binding to right side of quilt along 1 edge.

2. When you reach first corner, mark $^1/_4$" from corner of quilt top (**Fig. 31**).

3. Beginning approximately 10" from end of binding and using $^1/_4$" seam allowance, sew binding to quilt, backstitching at beginning of stitching and at mark (**Fig. 32**). Lift needle out of fabric and clip thread.

4. Fold binding as shown in **Figs. 33 - 34** and pin binding to adjacent side, matching raw edges. When reaching the next corner, mark $^1/_4$" from edge of quilt top.

Fig. 31

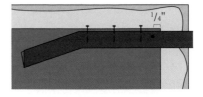

Fig. 32

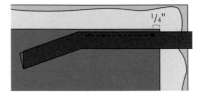

Fig. 33

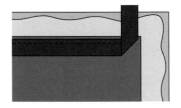

Fig. 34

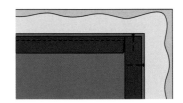

5 Backstitching at edge of quilt top, sew pinned binding to quilt (**Fig. 35**); backstitch at the next mark. Lift needle out of fabric and clip thread.

6 Continue sewing binding to quilt, stopping approximately 10" from starting point (**Fig. 36**).

7 Bring beginning and end of binding to center of opening and fold each end back, leaving a $^1/_4$" space between folds (**Fig. 37**). Finger-press folds.

8 Unfold ends of binding and draw a line across wrong side in finger-pressed crease. Draw a line through the lengthwise pressed fold of binding at same spot to create a cross mark. With edge of ruler at marked cross, line up 45° angle marking on ruler with one long side of binding. Draw a diagonal line from edge to edge. Repeat on remaining end, making sure that the two diagonal lines are angled the same way (**Fig. 38**).

Fig. 35

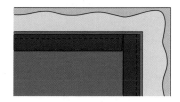

Fig. 36

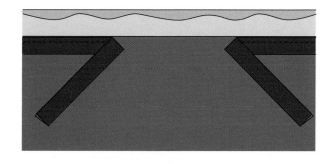

Fig. 37

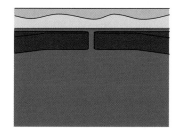

Fig. 38

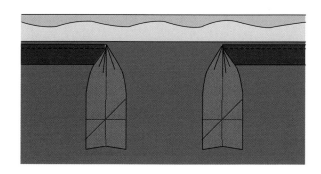

9 Matching right sides and diagonal lines, pin binding ends together at right angles (**Fig. 39**).

10 Machine stitch along diagonal line (**Fig. 40**), removing pins as you stitch.

11 Lay binding against quilt to double check that it is correct length.

12 Trim binding ends, leaving ¹/₄" seam allowance; press seam open. Stitch binding to quilt.

13 If using 2¹/₂"w binding (finished size ¹/₂"), trim backing and batting a scant ¹/₄" larger than quilt top so that batting and backing will fill the binding when it is folded over to quilt backing.

14 On 1 edge of quilt, fold binding over to quilt backing and pin pressed edge in place, covering stitching line (**Fig. 41**). On adjacent side, fold binding over, forming a mitered corner (**Fig. 42**). Repeat to pin remainder of binding in place.

15 Blindstitch binding to backing, taking care not to stitch through to front of quilt (**Fig. 43**).

Fig. 39

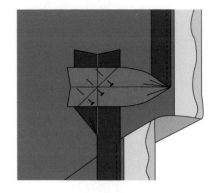

Fig. 40

Fig. 41

Fig. 42

Fig. 43

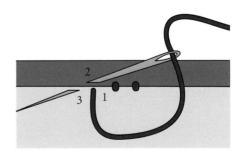

*If desired, you may add welting and/or a ruffle to the pillow top before sewing the pillow top and back together. Follow the instructions in **Perfect Pillow**, page 222, to construct desired pillow, and follow the steps below for adding welting or ruffle.*

ADDING WELTING TO PILLOW TOP

1 To make welting, use a bias strip of fabric to cover cord. Measure edge of pillow top and add 4". Measure circumference of cord and add 2". Cut a bias strip of fabric the determined measurement, piecing if necessary. (**Note:** *Purchased cording may be used instead of fabric covered welting. Skip to Step 3 to add purchased cording to pillow top.*)

2 Lay cord along center of bias strip on wrong side of fabric; fold strip over cord. Using a zipper foot, machine baste along length of strip close to cord. Trim seam allowance to ¼".

3 Matching raw edges and beginning and ending 3" from ends of welting, baste welting to right side of pillow top. To make turning corners easier, clip seam allowance of welting at pillow top corners.

4 Remove approximately 3" of seam at 1 end of welting; fold fabric away from cord. Trim remaining end of welting so that cord ends meet exactly (**Fig. 44**).

5 Fold short edge of welting fabric ½" to wrong side; fold fabric back over area where ends meet (**Fig. 45**).

6 Baste remainder of welting to pillow top close to cord (**Fig. 46**).

Fig. 44

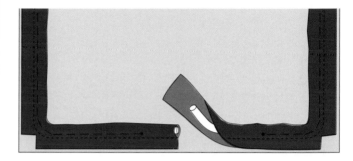

Fig. 45

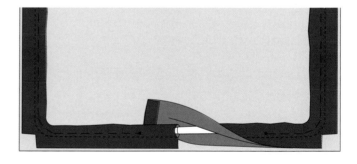

Fig. 46

ADDING RUFFLE TO PILLOW TOP

1 To determine *width* of fabric strip to cut for ruffle, multiply the desired finished width by 2 and add $1/2$". To determine *length* of fabric strip to cut, measure the edge of pillow top and multiply by $2^1/_2$. Cut strip to determined measurements, piecing as necessary.

2 Matching right sides, use a $1/4$" seam allowance to sew short edges of ruffle together to form a large circle; press seam allowance open. To form ruffle, fold along length with wrong sides together and raw edges matching; press.

3 To gather ruffle, place quilting thread $1/8$" from raw edge of ruffle. Using a medium-width zigzag stitch with medium stitch length, stitch over quilting thread, being careful not to catch quilting thread in stitching. Pull quilting thread, drawing up gathers to fit pillow top.

4 Matching raw edges, baste ruffle to right side of pillow top.

SIGNING AND DATING YOUR QUILT

A completed quilt is a work of art and should be signed and dated. There are many different ways to do this and numerous books on the subject. The label should reflect the style of the quilt, the occasion or person for which it was made, and the quilter's own particular talents. Following are suggestions for recording the history of the quilt or adding a sentiment for future generations.

- *Embroider quilter's name, date, and any additional information on quilt top or backing. Matching floss, such as cream floss on white border, will leave a subtle record. Bright or contrasting floss will make the information stand out.*

- *Make label from muslin and use permanent marker to write information. Use different colored permanent markers to make label more decorative. Stitch label to back of quilt.*

- *Use photo-transfer paper to add image to white or cream fabric label. Stitch label to back of quilt.*

- *Piece an extra block from quilt top pattern to use as label. Add information with permanent fabric pen. Stitch block to back of quilt.*